HANDS-ON GENAI, LLMS AND AI AGENTS.

A 100 Page Practical Guide to Master Generative AI, LLMs, and AI Agents by building practical applications.

by Aman Kharwal

BlueRose ONE.com
Stories Matter
NewDelhi • London

BLUEROSE PUBLISHERS
India | U.K.

BlueRose ONE.com
Stories Matter
NewDelhi • London

For permissions requests or inquiries regarding this publication, please contact:

BLUEROSE PUBLISHERS
www.BlueRoseONE.com
info@bluerosepublishers.com
+91 8882 898 898
+4407342408967

ISBN: 978-93-7542-223-5

First Edition: November 2025

Table of Contents

Preface

Welcome to the start of your journey into the most transformative technology of our decade.

Generative AI, Large Language Models (LLMs), and autonomous AI Agents are not just research curiosities anymore; they are the new foundation of software development. They are powering everything from intelligent coding assistants and personalized education platforms to complex, autonomous business processes. The shift isn't just about models getting bigger; it's about a new paradigm where software is written by the AI itself.

This book, "Hands-on GenAI, LLMs and AI Agents," is your practical, no-nonsense guide to mastering this new era. We're not going to spend time on high-level philosophical debates or complex, historical derivations you'll never use. Instead, we focus relentlessly on the **Intuition → Mathematics → Algorithmic Steps → Implementation Code** progression, ensuring you don't just know what to do, but deeply understand why you're doing it.

What This Book Will Teach You

From this book, my goal is to transform you from a developer who uses AI APIs into an AI Engineer who builds, deploys, and orchestrates production-grade GenAI applications. You will learn to:

- **Master Prompt Engineering and RAG:** Go beyond basic prompting to advanced techniques like Chain-of-Thought, Tree-of-Thought, and build powerful Retrieval-Augmented Generation (RAG) systems that ground LLMs in your proprietary data.

- **Fine-Tune and Customize LLMs:** Understand the mathematics and algorithms behind modern, efficient techniques like LoRA (Low-Rank Adaptation) and QLoRA so you can adapt open-source models (like those on Hugging Face) to your specific industry tasks, saving massive computational costs.

- **Architect Multi-Agent Systems:** Dive deep into the core concept of AI Agents, LLMs augmented with tools, memory, and planning, and learn how to design, build, and orchestrate complex AI Agent Systems where multiple agents collaborate to achieve sophisticated goals.

- **Implement Industry Best Practices:** Every example and project in this book is designed with a focus on real-world constraints: security, cost, latency, and scalability.

Development Environment Setup

Before diving into Chapter 1, let's ensure your workspace is ready. The barrier to entry for GenAI development is refreshingly low, but proper setup is crucial for avoiding dependency headaches.

1. The Right Editor: VS Code

We recommend using Visual Studio Code (VS Code). It offers the best experience for Python development, virtual environments, and notebook interaction.

2. Python and Virtual Environments

Never install packages globally! It leads to "dependency hell." The professional standard is to use a virtual environment for every project.

Install Python: Ensure you have Python 3.10 or later installed.

And, **create a Virtual Environment.** Open your terminal, navigate to your project directory, and run:

```
python -m venv venv
```

Also, make sure to activate the environment:

- **macOS/Linux: source venv/bin/activate**
- **Windows: .\venv\Scripts\activate**

Once activated, your terminal prompt will show **(venv)** at the start, indicating that any packages you install will be confined to this project. All of the code snippets in this book assume you are working within an active virtual environment.

Chapter 1 The Age of Generative AI

Welcome to the new frontier. If you've been in the AI world for a minute, you've likely seen the shift from predictive models, which tell you what will happen, to generative models, which literally create something new. This isn't just a technological upgrade; it's a paradigm shift that is reshaping industries.

I'm not just going to give you definitions. We'll dive into the core intuition, understand the practical mechanics, and get our hands dirty with code right out of the gate. Let's begin this journey toward becoming an advanced practitioner.

Understanding Generative AI in the Real World

At its core, Generative AI is about teaching a machine to understand the underlying distribution of a dataset and then sample from that learned distribution to produce novel, high-quality, and realistic outputs. Think of it less as a student memorizing facts and more as an artist developing a style.

They learn the rules of composition, colour, and form, and then use that knowledge to create something entirely new that still feels authentic.

Practical Examples and Real-World Impact

Content Creation

Earlier, a traditional AI model might classify a news article into Finance or Sports. Today, a Large Language Model can generate a comprehensive draft of a financial report or a marketing email based on a few bullet points.

Creative Design

Earlier, a computer vision system would detect if an image contains a cat or a dog. Today, models like DALL-E or Stable Diffusion can take a text prompt and render a stunning, original visual asset. This is creation, not recognition.

The key takeaway is that GenAI creates, while traditional AI primarily classifies or predicts.

Evolution: Traditional AI → Deep Learning → Generative AI

To appreciate where we are, we need to quickly anchor ourselves to where we came from. This evolution is defined by a change in what the model learns and how it represents that knowledge.

Era	Core Mechanism	Focus
Traditional AI/ML	Hand-engineered features, linear/simple models.	Prediction/Classification on structured data.
Deep Learning	Neural Networks with many hidden layers.	Representation Learning for unstructured data.
Generative AI	Massive-scale Deep Learning	Generation of novel, high-fidelity, complex outputs.

The critical bridge between Deep Learning and Generative AI is the concept of a latent space.

In Deep Learning, the hidden layers of a neural network compress high-dimensional input (like a megapixel image) into a much smaller, dense vector representation. This is the latent space.

In GenAI, this latent space is so well-structured, meaning similar concepts are mapped to nearby points, that we can start to navigate it. By sampling a new, random point in this space and decoding it, we can produce a novel output that is statistically indistinguishable from the training data.

Foundation Models vs. Fine-Tuned Models

This distinction is fundamental for building real-world AI applications.

It's the difference between buying a fully-equipped professional kitchen and customizing it for your specific restaurant's menu.

Foundation Models

These are massive, general-purpose models (like GPT-4, PaLM, or Llama) trained on vast, diverse, and internet-scale data. They acquire a broad range of general skills, knowledge, and reasoning capabilities.

They know a little bit about coding, history, poetry, and summarizing text, all because they've seen so much data.

Their use cases include:

1. **Zero-Shot/Few-Shot Learning:** Prompting the model to perform a task it wasn't explicitly trained for. For example: "Translate this Finnish poem into English."
2. **Broad Content Generation:** Chatbots, general Q&A, and summarizing documents across different domains.

Fine-Tuned Models

A Foundation Model that has been further trained (fine-tuned) on a smaller, task-specific dataset to specialize in a particular domain or task. They take the general knowledge of the Foundation Model and hone it to achieve high accuracy and relevance for a specific, narrow vertical.

They speak the jargon of a particular industry perfectly.

Their use cases include:

1. **Domain Expertise:** Training a large language model on thousands of pages of a company's knowledge base to create a highly accurate bot.
2. **Style and Tone:** Adjusting a model's output to exclusively use a specific brand's voice and terminology.

Feature	Foundation Models	Fine-Tuned Models
Data Size	Massive (Terabytes)	Small to Medium (Gigabytes)
Cost	Very High Training Cost	Low to Moderate Training Cost
Practitioner Insight	We usually **use them** (via API or hosted models).	We usually **build them** (from a base model).

Overview of Text, Image, and Multimodal GenAI Systems

Generative AI is not one thing; it's a family of powerful techniques applied across different data types.

1. Text Generation (LLMs)

The core idea here is to **model the probability of the next token** (word, sub-word, or character) given all the preceding tokens. This is essentially a sophisticated next-word predictor.

For example, "The cat sat on the [mat]."

Here, the model calculates the probability of every possible next word and selects one. By doing this millions of times, it generates coherent prose.

2. Image Generation (Diffusion Models)

These models are based on a process of gradual denoising.

Let's say an image is perfectly clear. Now, gradually add noise (static) until it's pure randomness. A Diffusion Model learns to reverse this process: it starts with pure noise and iteratively removes the noise to reveal the original image. By using a text prompt to condition this denoising process, it can generate an image corresponding to the prompt.

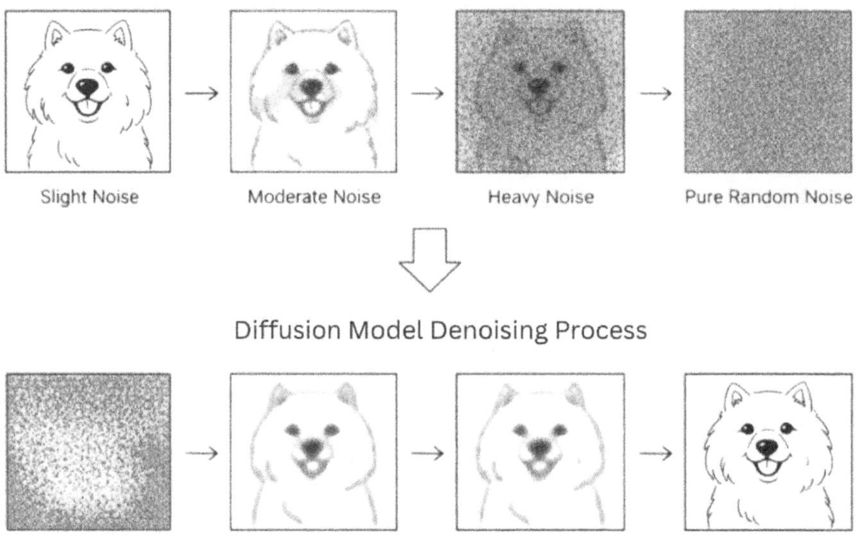

3. Multimodal Generation

The core idea here is to seamlessly process and generate across multiple data types (e.g., text → image, image → text, text and image → text).

Here, a single, large model is trained to understand the relationship between data types. For example, the model learns that the phrase "red car" corresponds to the visual pixels of a red car. This shared understanding (or embedding space) is the key.

This is arguably the most powerful frontier. Models like GPT-4o or Gemini can take an image of a handwritten note, understand the handwriting, read the contents, and then summarize it in text—an end-to-end multimodal process.

Mini Project: Generating Creative Text with Hugging Face

This is where we will learn some concepts by building.

We'll use the Hugging Face ecosystem, which is the industry standard for deploying and experimenting with GenAI models. Specifically, we'll use the transformers library and a small but capable LLM to get our feet wet with text generation.

Step 1: Setting up the Environment

You'll need Python and the Hugging Face transformers library installed.

```
pip install transformers torch
```

Step 2: The Intuition of Generation

When we call a model to generate text, we're not just asking for the next word. We're running an iterative process that involves sampling. If we always picked the most likely next word (a process called greedy decoding), the text would become repetitive and boring.

To introduce creativity, we use sampling techniques.

We will use **Top-k or Top-p (Nucleus) sampling**, which is the secret sauce for creative GenAI:

1. **Top-k:** Only considers the top k most likely next words.
2. **Top-p (Nucleus):** Considers the smallest set of words whose cumulative probability exceeds a threshold p (e.g., 95% probability). It dynamically adjusts the number of considered words, leading to better, more human-like variety.

Step 3: Implementation Code

We'll use DistilGPT2, a smaller, faster version of GPT-2, for quick execution.

```
from transformers import pipeline

# 1. Initialize the Text Generation Pipeline
# This is the easiest way to get started with a pre-trained model
generator = pipeline("text-generation", model="distilgpt2")

# 2. Define the Prompt
prompt = "The AI agent quickly analyzed the data stream, and its core decision was to"

# 3. Generate the Text with Sampling Parameters
# We'll use parameters to make the output more creative and less repetitive.
output = generator(
    prompt,
    max_length=100,  # Stop after 100 tokens (words/sub-words)
    num_return_sequences=1,  # Generate 1 sequence
    do_sample=True,  # Crucial: enable sampling for non-greedy generation
    top_k=50,  # Consider only the top 50 likely words
    top_p=0.95,  # The Nucleus Sampling threshold
    temperature=0.75, # Controls randomness: higher = crazier, lower = safer
)
```

```
# Continued
# 4. Print the Result
print("Prompt")
print(prompt)
print("\n Generated Output")
# The output is a list of dictionaries, we extract the generated_text key
print(output[0]['generated_text'])
```

Example Output:

```
Prompt
The AI agent quickly analyzed the data stream, and its core decision was to
Generated

Output
The AI agent quickly analyzed the data stream, and its core decision was to use
the same method...
```

You've just taken a Foundation Model, applied core generation principles (sampling), and produced a high-quality, creative output.

This hands-on step is the essence of modern GenAI practice: selecting the right model, understanding the decoding process, and tuning parameters to achieve the desired creative outcome.

Summary

So, Generative AI is the capability of machines to create novel outputs (text, images, code, etc.) by learning the underlying distribution of data, moving beyond traditional AI's focus on classification and prediction.

Key takeaways from this chapter:

- **GenAI** is the shift from models that predict to models that create. Real-world applications include content creation, drug discovery, and creative design.

- **Foundation Models** are large, general-purpose models (e.g., Llama, GPT-4) trained on vast, diverse data, serving as the versatile jack-of-all-trades.

- **Fine-Tuned Models** specialize by taking a Foundation Model and training it further on a smaller, domain-specific dataset, becoming masters of a narrow task (e.g., legal or medical text generation).

The chapter sets the stage for understanding the shift from predictive to creative AI and provides the foundational terminology and practical context necessary for the hands-on journey ahead.

Chapter 2 Inside Large Language Models

The journey of a Large Language Model, from a raw string of text to a coherent response, is a carefully orchestrated process built on three fundamental pillars: **Tokenization, the Transformer Architecture, and the Attention Mechanism.**

Tokenization: The Language-to-Math Translator

Think of tokenization as the very first translator in the pipeline. A computer doesn't understand words like "apple" or "intelligence." It only understands numbers. Tokenization is the process of breaking down raw text into smaller, meaningful units—called tokens—and mapping each one to a unique ID (a number) that the model can process.

In human language, our basic unit is a word. In LLMs, a token can be a word, a part of a word (a subword), or even a single character.

For Example, in the sentence: "Unbelievable efficiency."
A simple tokenization might be:

"Unbelievable" , "efficiency"

But, a more common, modern Subword Tokenization approach (Byte Pair Encoding - BPE is a popular one) for the same sentence might be:

"Unbel","ie","vable","effici","ency"

But, Why Subwords?

Instead of having a giant vocabulary with an entry for every obscure word, subword tokenization allows the model to construct that word from smaller, common pieces ("pneumono," "ultra," etc.). This dramatically shrinks the vocabulary size while still being able to represent any word.

It creates smaller, shared vocabulary pieces across different languages that are more memory-efficient and generalize better.

This is how Tokenization Works:

1. **Text Cleanup:** Normalize text (lowercase, remove extra spaces).
2. **Splitting:** Apply rules to split the text into tokens.
3. **Mapping:** Look up each token in the model's vocabulary to get its unique integer ID.
4. **Output:** A sequence of integer IDs that now represent the input text, ready for the mathematical model.

The Transformer: The Blueprint for Sequence Processing

Before the Transformer (introduced in the landmark 2017 paper Attention Is All You Need), models like RNNs and LSTMs processed text sequentially, like reading a book one word after the next.

This was slow and struggled to remember things from the very beginning of a long text (the "vanishing gradient" problem).

The Transformer revolutionized this by saying:

"Forget sequence! Let's process the entire input at once and let every word look at every other word to decide its own meaning."

To understand better, imagine an architect designing a building. Instead of building one floor at a time and forgetting what the ground floor looked like, the architect reviews the entire blueprint simultaneously, allowing the roof supports to know exactly what the foundation supports are doing.

Traditional Approach

Modern Approach

The Transformer architecture is typically composed of a stack of identical layers, each containing two main sub-layers:

1. **Multi-Head Self-Attention:** Where the context happens.
2. **Feed-Forward Network:** Where the model processes the context found by the attention layer.

Attention: The Mechanism of Context

Attention is the LLM's ability to dynamically focus.

When you read the sentence, "The bank was so muddy the dog jumped into the water," how do you know if "bank" means a financial institution or the side of a river?

You **pay attention** to the words around it, like "muddy" and "water."

The Self-Attention mechanism in a large language model does the same thing mathematically. For every single token in a sentence, it calculates an Attention Score between that token and every other token (including itself).

This score quantifies how much "focus" or "importance" the current token should place on another token to fully understand its own meaning in that context.

The Core Mathematics (Conceptual): Query, Key, and Value

For every token, the model computes three vectors:

1. **Query (Q):** What am I looking for?
2. **Key (K):** What do I have to offer?
3. **Value (V)**: What information should I give?

The Attention Score between two tokens is calculated by taking the **dot product** of the Q of the current token and the K of another token.

$$\text{Attention}(Q, K, V) = \text{softmax}\left((Q K^T) / \sqrt{d_k} \right) V$$

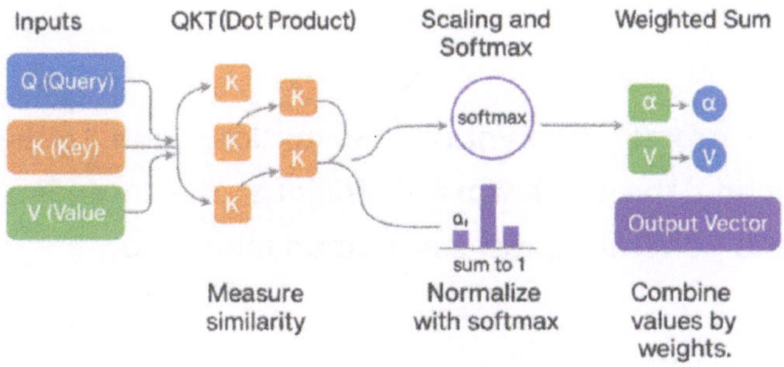

The term $\mathbf{QK^T}$ calculates the raw compatibility (the attention score) between all queries and keys.

The division by $\sqrt{\mathbf{d_K}}$ (the dimension of the key vectors) is a scaling factor to prevent the dot products from getting too large, which can push the softmax function into regions where its gradient is tiny, hindering learning.

The softmax turns these raw scores into probability-like weights that sum to 1. Finally, multiplying by the **V** vectors is like saying: "Take the information (Value) from every other token, but scale it (weight it) by how relevant its Key was to my Query."

The output for the current token is a new, contextualized vector, a weighted sum of all the Value vectors, effectively packing the entire sentence's context right into the representation of that single word.

Pretraining and Fine-tuning: Building and Shaping the Brain

LLMs are developed in two distinct, sequential phases that mirror how a human learns a general skill and then specializes.

Pretraining

Pretraining is like a motivated student reading every book in a massive library (Wikipedia, Common Crawl, etc.) over several years.

Such models learn **grammar, syntax, semantics, and general world knowledge** by predicting the next word in trillions of sentences. In simple words, they absorb the general patterns of human language.

How Pretrained Models Work:
Let's take the example of the most common pretraining task: Next Token Prediction (or Masked Language Modelling, depending on the model type).

The model is fed a sequence of tokens:

"The","capital","of","France","is", * * ?

It is trained to output a high probability for the correct next token (e.g., "Paris"). The model is repeatedly penalized (Loss) when its prediction is wrong and rewarded when it's right, iteratively adjusting billions of weights.

Pretraining is computationally massive. This is where the cost and time commitment truly spike, often requiring thousands of high-end GPUs for months. The resulting model is a Generalist Language Model; it knows a lot about language, but isn't yet tailored for a specific, helpful task like answering questions or following instructions.

Fine-tuning

Fine-tuning is taking that highly educated, generalist student and enrolling them in a one-month intensive training program to become a specialist, like a personal assistant.

The goal here is to take the pretrained general knowledge and align the model's behaviour to a specific task or a desired set of instructions, often emphasizing helpfulness, harmlessness, and honesty.

There are two key Fine-Tuning stages:

1. **Supervised Fine-Tuning (SFT):** The model is trained on a relatively small, high-quality dataset of prompt-response pairs (e.g., "Prompt: Summarize this text." → "Response: Here is the summary..."). This phase teaches the model to adopt the desired instruction-following format and **style.**
2. **Reinforcement Learning from Human Feedback (RLHF):** This is the crucial alignment phase.

Fine-tuning, especially with techniques like LoRA (Low-Rank Adaptation), is much cheaper and faster than pretraining. It often involves updating only a small fraction of the model's weights, making it an accessible step for practitioners to customize an LLM for proprietary data or niche tasks.

Embeddings and Vector Representations: The DNA of Meaning

An Embedding is a compact, dense vector (a list of numbers, like [0.23,−1.5,0.04,...]) that numerically represents a piece of information, whether it's a word, a sentence, or an entire document.

Imagine the model creating a massive, multi-dimensional "Map of Meaning." On this map:

1. **Semantically similar words are placed close together.**
2. **Words that are semantically different are placed far apart.**

For example, the vector for "King" might be closer to "Queen" and "Man" than it is to "Banana."

The famous vector relationship:

$$\text{Vector(King)} - \text{Vector(Man)} + \text{Vector(Woman)} \approx \text{Vector(Queen)}$$

This demonstrates that the vector space captures linear relationships between concepts. The direction and distance between two vectors on this map encode their relationship.

But, Why Embeddings? The Technical Need:
Standard **One-Hot Encoding** (where 'cat' is [0,0,1,0,...] and 'dog' is [0,1,0,0,...]) makes every word equidistant from all others, providing no information about meaning.

Embeddings solve this by:

1. **Capturing Context:** Unlike static word embeddings (like the old Word2Vec), Transformer embeddings are contextual. The embedding for the word "bank" changes depending on whether the sentence is about a river bank or a money bank.
2. **Reducing Dimensionality:** They represent a massive vocabulary (millions of words) using a manageable vector (often 768 or 1024 dimensions), which is crucial for efficient computation.

The primary way we use embeddings in advanced AI is for **Semantic Search or Retrieval-Augmented Generation (RAG).** Instead of searching a database for an exact keyword match, we use an input query's embedding to search for documents with nearby embeddings (meaning the document is semantically similar), yielding much more relevant results.

Hands-on: Generating Sentence Embeddings with Sentence Transformers

We're going to put this concept into immediate practice.

The Sentence Transformers library (built on PyTorch and Hugging Face Transformers) is the industry-standard toolkit for generating high-quality, dense sentence and paragraph embeddings.

Algorithmic Steps We Use:

1. **Model Selection:** Choose an embedding model (like, **all-MiniLM-L6-v2**), which is optimized for sentence-level tasks.
2. **Tokenization:** The model internally tokenizes the input sentences.
3. **Transformer Pass:** The tokens pass through the Transformer model.
4. **Pooling:** Since the Transformer outputs an embedding vector for each token, we need one vector for the entire sentence. Pooling aggregates all token vectors into a single, fixed-size sentence vector.
5. **Normalization:** The final vector is usually normalized (its length is set to 1) so that vector similarity (like Cosine Similarity) only depends on the angle between the vectors, not their magnitude.

Implementation using Python

We'll use a simple example to show how two semantically close sentences have very close vector representations.

First, import the necessary libraries:

```
from sentence_transformers import SentenceTransformer
import numpy as np
from sklearn.metrics.pairwise import cosine_similarity
```

Step 1: Model Selection and Loading:

```
# 'all-MiniLM-L6-v2' is small, fast, and very effective.
print("Loading the Sentence Transformer model...")
model = SentenceTransformer('all-MiniLM-L6-v2')
print("Model loaded successfully.")
```

Step 2: Define our input sentences:

```
sentences = [
    "A dog is chasing a bright red ball on a sunny green field.",
    "The canine pursues a crimson sphere across the lawn.",
    "I'm planning to bake an apple pie for the picnic next weekend.",
    "A new laptop was purchased from the tech store today."
]
```

Step 3: Generate Embeddings:

```
print("\nGenerating embeddings for the sentences...")
embeddings = model.encode(sentences)
```

Now, we will look at the shape and size of the vectors:

```
print(f"Shape of the embeddings tensor: {embeddings.shape}")
print(f"Embedding dimension (d_k): {embeddings.shape[1]}")
print(f"Sample of the first embedding vector: {embeddings[0][:5]}...")
```

```
Shape of the embeddings tensor: (4, 384)
Embedding dimension (d_k): 384
Sample of the first embedding vector: [ 0.06738607 -0.03597434 0.009422 -0.00215971
0.04763954]...
```

This output confirms that the model successfully processed four input sentences (indicated by the (4,384) tensor shape). Each sentence was converted into a dense, numerical vector representation or embedding consisting of 384 floating-point numbers.

This 384-dimensional vector mathematically encodes the semantic meaning of its corresponding sentence, allowing the model to determine relationships between texts (like similarity or difference) by measuring the distance or angle between these vectors in the 384D space.

The sample values like **[0.067,−0.035,...]** are just the beginning elements of the vector that represent the sentence's meaning.

Step 4: Calculate Semantic Similarity (Cosine Similarity)

Now, we will compare the first sentence (S1) with the others:

```
# Calculate the cosine similarity matrix for all pairs
similarity_matrix = cosine_similarity(embeddings)

# Extract and display the key similarities
S1_S2_sim = similarity_matrix[0, 1]
S1_S3_sim = similarity_matrix[0, 2]
S1_S4_sim = similarity_matrix[0, 3]

print("\n--- Semantic Similarity Analysis (Cosine Score: 1.0 = Identical, 0.0 =
Unrelated) ---")

print(f"Similarity (S1 vs S2 - Similar Meaning): {S1_S2_sim:.4f}")
print(f"Similarity (S1 vs S3 - Different Meaning): {S1_S3_sim:.4f}")
print(f"Similarity (S1 vs S4 - Different Meaning): {S1_S4_sim:.4f}")
```

```
--- Semantic Similarity Analysis (Cosine Score: 1.0 = Identical, 0.0 = Unrelated) ---
Similarity (S1 vs S2 - Similar Meaning): 0.5318
Similarity (S1 vs S3 - Different Meaning): 0.0127
Similarity (S1 vs S4 - Different Meaning): 0.0888
```

The Cosine Similarity score of 0.5318 between Sentence 1 (S1) and Sentence 2 (S2) indicates they are highly related in meaning, as the vectors point in a similar direction (closer to the maximum score of 1.0).

Conversely, the extremely low scores of 0.0127 (S1 vs S3) and 0.0888 (S1 vs S4) confirm that S1 is semantically distant and essentially unrelated to S3 and S4, validating the embeddings' ability to quantitatively distinguish between similar and dissimilar text.

This hands-on exercise is the foundation of building AI Agents that can use Knowledge Retrieval. Understanding this output means you now know how LLMs translate words into searchable, quantifiable meaning!

Summary

In this chapter, we understood LLMs by focusing on their core mechanics and lifecycle.

We established that LLMs process language by first using Tokenization to convert text into numerical IDs (often using efficient subwords). The core engine is the Transformer Architecture, which utilizes the Self-Attention mechanism. Attention allows every word to dynamically weigh the importance of every other word in the sequence, creating contextualized vector representations (Embeddings) crucial for understanding meaning.

The model's development occurs in two phases: massive, generalist Pretraining (Next Token Prediction) and specialized Fine-tuning (SFT and RLHF) to align its behavior for specific tasks like instruction-following.

Finally, we explored how Embeddings represent meaning in a multi-dimensional space, enabling practical applications like Semantic Search, which was demonstrated through a hands-on guide using the Sentence Transformers library.

Chapter 3 Building a Custom Chatbot using LLMs

In the last chapter, we understood the architecture of Large Language Models. Now, it's time to roll up our sleeves and start building with them.

Ever wished you could have a conversation with your company's 100-page annual report or get a quick summary of a dense research paper without reading the whole thing?

That's precisely what we're going to build in this chapter.

We'll start by mastering the art of **communication with LLMs through prompt engineering**.

Then, we'll learn to control the model's personality, from strictly factual to wildly creative, by tuning its core parameters.

Finally, we'll put it all together in a hands-on project by building a custom chatbot that can read any PDF you upload and answer questions about its contents.

Let's get started.

The Art of Conversation: Prompt Engineering Essentials

Think of a Large Language Model as a brilliant, hyper-literate intern who has read almost the entire internet. They're incredibly knowledgeable but also extremely literal. If you give them a vague instruction like, "Tell me about dogs," you'll get a generic, unfocused encyclopedia entry.

But if you ask, "Explain the key differences in temperament between a Golden Retriever and a German Shepherd for a first-time dog owner," you'll get a precise, useful, and context-aware response.

Prompt engineering is the craft of designing these precise inputs to get the exact outputs you want. It's less about coding and more about applied linguistics and psychology. You're not programming the model in Python; you're guiding its "thought process" with carefully chosen words. A well-crafted prompt is the difference between a useless chatbot and a powerful AI assistant.

Here are the core principles you need to internalize:

1. **Be Specific and Clear:** Avoid ambiguity; the more detailed your request, the better the result.
2. **Provide Context:** Give the model all the background information it needs to answer your question. Don't make it guess.
3. **Assign a Persona:** Tell the model who it should be. This is a powerful trick to frame its tone, style, and knowledge base.
4. **Use Examples (Few-Shot Prompting):** Instead of just telling the model what to do, show it with a few examples.
5. **Add Constraints:** Clearly define the boundaries for the output. Tell the model the desired length, format, or things to avoid.

Let's see this in action with some good vs. bad prompts.

Scenario 1: Summarizing a Technical Article

👎 **Bad Prompt:** *"Summarize this."*

It's lazy and vague. Summarize for whom? How long? What's the key focus? The model has to guess, and it will likely produce a generic, bland summary.

👍 **Good Prompt:**

"You are a science journalist. Summarize the following article for a non-technical audience. Your summary should be a single paragraph of about 100 words. Start with a catchy hook and focus on the real-world implications of the research. Avoid jargon at all costs."

It assigns a persona (science journalist), defines the audience (non-technical), provides constraints (single paragraph, ~100 words), and gives clear instructions on the focus (real-world implications).

Scenario 2: Generating Code

👎 **Bad Prompt:** *"Write a Python function for sorting."*

Sorting what? A list of numbers? Strings? Objects? What algorithm should it use? This prompt is an invitation for the model to give you the most basic, and possibly irrelevant, sorting function.

👍 **Good Prompt:**

"You are an expert Python developer who writes clean, efficient, and well-documented code.

Write a Python function called 'sort_by_last_letter' that takes a list of strings as input. The function should sort the list in-place based on the last letter of each string, in ascending alphabetical order.

Also, provide two simple examples of its usage with 'assert' statements to verify correctness."

See the difference?

Mastering these principles will fundamentally change how you interact with and build upon LLMs.

Controlling Creativity: Temperature, Top-k, and Top-p

When an LLM generates text, it's essentially playing a game of what's the most likely next word at every single step. After processing the input "The sun is shining and the birds are...", the model calculates a probability score for every word in its vocabulary. "Singing" might have a high probability, "flying" a slightly lower one, and "coding" a very, very low one.

How the model chooses from this list of probable words is what determines its "personality." Does it always pick the most obvious, highest-probability word? Or does it sometimes take a chance on a less likely, more interesting word?

Temperature, Top-k, and Top-p are the knobs we can turn to control this creative risk-taking. They don't change the model's knowledge, but they dramatically change its output behaviour.

Temperature

Think of temperature as the "randomness" or "creativity" dial.

1. **Low Temperature (0.1, 0.2):** The model becomes very conservative and deterministic. It will almost always pick the highest-probability word. The output will be predictable, focused, and a bit boring. This is great for factual tasks.
2. **High Temperature (0.8, 1.0):** The model gets more adventurous. It's more willing to pick less likely words, leading to more diverse, creative, and sometimes surprising outputs. Ideal for brainstorming or creative writing.

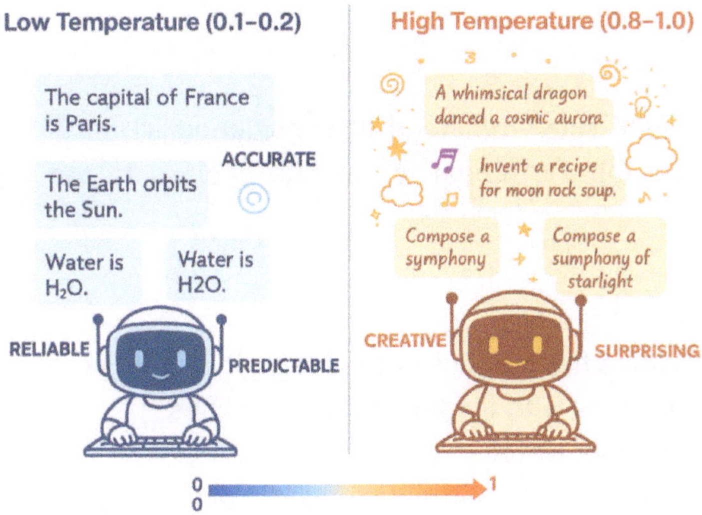

Temperature works by adjusting the probability distribution of the possible next words before sampling. The model first calculates a raw score for each word, called a logit. Before converting these logits into probabilities using a softmax function, it divides them by the temperature value (T).

The probability P_i for a word i with logit z_i is calculated as:

$$P_i = e^{(z_i / T)} / \Sigma_j e^{(z_j / T)}$$

A low temperature (T<1) makes the differences between high and low scores more extreme, so the model becomes more confident in its top choice. A high temperature (T>1) flattens the distribution, making the less likely words more competitive.

Practical Tuning Insights:

1. For **code generation or factual Q&A**, use a low temperature like 0.2. You want predictable and accurate results.
2. For **writing marketing copy, brainstorming ideas, or creating a story**, use a higher temperature like 0.75 or 0.9. You want creativity and diversity.

Top-k Sampling

This technique is quite simple. Instead of considering all 50,000+ possible next words, we just tell the model to limit its choices to the top k most probable words.

Algorithmic Steps:

1. The model calculates the probability for every word in its vocabulary.
2. It identifies the k words with the highest probabilities.
3. It throws away all other words.
4. It then samples a word from this reduced pool, using their adjusted probabilities.

For example, if k=3 and the top words are "singing" (70%), "chirping" (20%), and "flying" (10%), the model will only choose one of these three and will completely ignore "coding," no matter how high the temperature is.

Practical Consideration: top_k is a simple way to prevent the model from picking truly bizarre words. However, it can be too restrictive. Sometimes the probability distribution is sharp (one word is very likely), and sometimes it's flat (many words are equally likely). A fixed k doesn't adapt to this. This brings us to a better alternative.

Top-p (Nucleus) Sampling

Top-p is the more intelligent and widely used cousin of Top-k. Instead of picking a fixed number of words, you pick a cumulative probability threshold. You instruct the model to consider the most probable words, starting from the top, until their combined probability reaches a threshold p.

This set of words is called the "nucleus."

Algorithmic Steps:

1. The model calculates the probability for every word, sorted from most to least likely.
2. It starts adding words to a list, one by one, while summing their probabilities.
3. As soon as the cumulative probability of the list is greater than or equal to p, it stops.
4. The model then samples a word only from this dynamically created list (the nucleus).

For example:

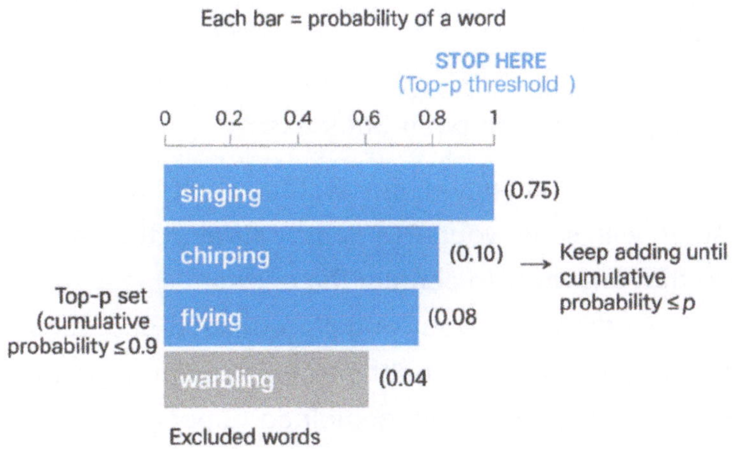

Here, the model will only consider "singing," "chirping," and "flying" because their combined probability (0.93) is the first to exceed our p of 0.9. The size of the nucleus is dynamic. If one word has a 95% probability, the nucleus will only contain that one word, making the output very predictable. If many words have low probabilities, the nucleus will be larger, allowing for more diversity.

Top-p is generally preferred over Top-k. A value of p=0.9 or p=0.95 is a fantastic starting point for most tasks, offering a great balance between creativity and coherence. **When you use top_p, leave top_k unset.**

Hands-on: Building a "Chat with your PDF" Bot

Alright, theory class is over. Let's build something genuinely useful. We're going to create a Python application that lets you upload a PDF and ask questions about it.

Introducing the RAG Framework

We won't be retraining a massive LLM, which is incredibly expensive. Instead, we'll use a powerful and efficient technique called Retrieval-Augmented Generation (RAG).

Think of RAG as giving the LLM an open-book exam.

1. **Retrieval:** When you ask a question, our system won't immediately talk to the LLM. First, it will scan your PDF and retrieve the most relevant snippets of text that are likely to contain the answer.
2. **Augmentation:** It will then take your original question and augment it by pasting the retrieved text snippets right into the prompt as context.
3. **Generation:** Finally, it will hand this combined super-prompt (context + question) to the LLM and say, "Using only the information I just gave you, answer this question."

This approach is fantastic because it forces the LLM to base its answers on the actual content of your document, dramatically reducing the chances of it making things up or hallucinating.

Algorithmic Steps & Implementation

Let's build this step-by-step. Make sure you have these necessary libraries installed:

```
pip install transformers torch sentence-transformers pypdf faiss-cpu
```

1. **transformers:** For accessing Hugging Face models.
2. **torch:** The backend for our ML models.
3. **sentence-transformers:** For creating high-quality text embeddings.
4. **pypdf:** To read and extract text from our PDF files.
5. **faiss-cpu:** A library from Meta AI for efficient similarity search in our vector store.

Step 1: Load and Chunk the Document

LLMs have a **limited context window (the amount of text they can look at once).** We can't feed it a 100-page PDF. So, we'll load the PDF and split its text into small, overlapping chunks:

```
import pypdf
from transformers import AutoTokenizer, AutoModelForSeq2SeqLM
from sentence_transformers import SentenceTransformer
import numpy as np
import faiss

# Document Loading and Chunking
def load_and_chunk_pdf(file_path, chunk_size=512, overlap=50):
    """Loads a PDF, extracts text, and splits it into chunks."""
    print("Loading and chunking PDF...")
    reader = pypdf.PdfReader(file_path)
    text = ""
    for page in reader.pages:
        text += page.extract_text() or ""

    # Simple chunking logic
    chunks = []
    for i in range(0, len(text), chunk_size - overlap):
        chunks.append(text[i:i + chunk_size])
    print(f"Created {len(chunks)} chunks.")
    return chunks

# Example usage:
# Make sure you have a PDF file named 'sample.pdf' in your directory
pdf_chunks = load_and_chunk_pdf('sample.pdf')
```

We used pypdf to read the document page by page. Then, we implemented a basic sliding window logic to create chunks. The overlap is crucial; it ensures that a sentence isn't awkwardly cut off between two chunks, preserving semantic context.

Step 2: Embed Chunks and Store in a Vector Database

Next, we need to convert our text chunks into numerical vectors so we can mathematically compare them for similarity. We'll use a sentence-transformer model for this. These embeddings will then be stored in a FAISS index, which is essentially a super-fast database for searching vectors:

```
# Embedding Model
print("Loading embedding model...")
embedding_model = SentenceTransformer('all-MiniLM-L6-v2')

# Create Embeddings and Vector Store (FAISS)
def create_vector_store(chunks, model):
    """Embeds chunks and stores them in a FAISS index."""
    print("Creating embeddings and vector store...")
    embeddings = model.encode(chunks, convert_to_tensor=True)
    embeddings_np = embeddings.cpu().numpy()

    # FAISS index setup
    dimension = embeddings_np.shape[1]
    index = faiss.IndexFlatL2(dimension)
    index.add(embeddings_np)
    print("Vector store created successfully.")
    return index

vector_store = create_vector_store(pdf_chunks, embedding_model)
```

```
Loading embedding model...
Creating embeddings and vector store...
Vector store created successfully.
```

Here, we are loading 'all-MiniLM-L6-v2', a popular and efficient model for creating sentence embeddings. The encode function turns our list of text chunks into a list of 384-dimensional vectors. We then created a simple FAISS index (IndexFlatL2 is a basic but effective choice) and added our vectors to it.

Step 3: Retrieve Relevant Chunks

This is the "Retrieval" part of RAG. We'll create a function that takes a user's question, embeds it using the same model, and then uses our FAISS index to find the most similar chunks from the PDF:

```
# Retrieval Logic
def retrieve_relevant_chunks(query, index, chunks, model, top_k=3):
    """Finds the most relevant chunks for a given query."""
    print(f"Retrieving top {top_k} chunks for query: '{query}'")
    query_embedding = model.encode([query], convert_to_tensor=True).cpu().numpy()

    # Search the FAISS index
    distances, indices = index.search(query_embedding, top_k)

    # Return the actual text chunks
    return [chunks[i] for i in indices[0]]
```

Here, we embed the user's query. The index.search() function is the core of our retrieval. It takes the query vector and finds the top_k closest vectors in the index, returning their indices. We then used these indices to pull out the original text chunks.

Step 4: Augment Prompt and Generate Answer

Now, we'll load a generative LLM, construct our super-prompt containing the retrieved context and the question, and ask the model to generate an answer:

```
# Generation Logic
print("Loading generative LLM...")
# Using a smaller, manageable model for local execution
llm_tokenizer = AutoTokenizer.from_pretrained("google/flan-t5-base")
llm_model = AutoModelForSeq2SeqLM.from_pretrained("google/flan-t5-base")

def generate_answer(query, context_chunks):
    """Builds a prompt and generates an answer using the LLM."""
    print("Generating answer...")
    context = " ".join(context_chunks)

    prompt = f"""
    Please answer the following question based only on the provided context.
    If the context does not contain the answer, say "I don't have enough
information from the document to answer this."
```

```
    Context:
    {context}

    Question:
    {query}

    Answer:
    """

    inputs = llm_tokenizer(prompt, return_tensors="pt",
    max_length=1024, truncation=True)
    outputs = llm_model.generate(**inputs, max_length=200,
    temperature=0.1, top_p=0.95)

    return llm_tokenizer.decode(outputs[0], skip_special_tokens=True)

# Main Chatbot Logic
def ask_chatbot(query):
    """End-to-end function to chat with the PDF."""
    retrieved_chunks = retrieve_relevant_chunks(query,
                                               vector_store,
                                               pdf_chunks, embedding_model)
    answer = generate_answer(query, retrieved_chunks)
    return answer
```

Here, we loaded flan-t5-base, a solid instruction-tuned model.

Our generate_answer function creates a carefully crafted prompt template. This is crucial prompt engineering! We explicitly tell the model to only use the provided context. We then tokenized this prompt and passed it to llm_model.generate().

Notice **we're using a low temperature** because we want a factual, non-creative answer based on the text.

Sample Interaction

I am using a sample PDF based on research by Apple on LLMs. This paper introduces a groundbreaking finding in the study of Large Language Models (LLMs): the existence of "super weights."

Now, let's run our chatbot and ask some questions from our document:

```
user_question = "How does the paper propose to identify super weights in a data-free way?"

final_answer = ask_chatbot(user_question)

print("\n--- Chatbot Response ---")
print(final_answer)
```

```
Retrieving top 3 chunks for query: 'How does the paper propose to identify super weights in a data-free way?'
Generating answer...

--- Chatbot Response ---
Detecting the spikes in the down proj inputs and outputs distributions across the layers
```

Our chatbot correctly extracted the information and answered the question accurately, all without being explicitly trained on that paper. It learned on the fly using the context we provided.

Now, we've gone from theory to a fully functional, real-world application. You now understand how to communicate with, control, and augment LLMs to build custom solutions.

Summary

In this chapter, we covered how to build a custom chatbot that understands your documents. First, we covered prompt engineering, showing you how to write clear and specific instructions to get the best results from a Large Language Model (LLM).

Next, we covered how to control the LLM's creativity and factual accuracy by tuning key parameters like Temperature, Top-p, and Top-k.

Finally, we went through a hands-on project to build a "Chat with your PDF" bot using the powerful Retrieval-Augmented Generation (RAG) technique, which allows the LLM to answer questions based on the content of an uploaded file.

Chapter 4 Fine-Tuning and Adapting LLMs

Welcome to Chapter 4! So far, we've treated Large Language Models like powerful, off-the-shelf tools. We've prompted them, chained them, and given them access to external knowledge.

But what happens when the general-purpose nature of a pre-trained model isn't quite enough? What if you need the model to adopt a specific personality, master a niche vocabulary, or learn a completely new skill?

That's when you need to adapt the model itself. This chapter is all about moving from being a model user to a model trainer. We'll explore the two primary ways to specialize a model:

1. **providing it with external knowledge at runtime (RAG)**
2. **and fundamentally changing its behaviour by updating its weights (fine-tuning).**

We'll tackle the crucial strategic decision of when to use which method. Then, we'll dive into the revolutionary techniques like **PEFT and LoRA** that have made fine-tuning accessible to everyone. Finally, we'll get our hands dirty with a complete, step-by-step guide to fine-tuning your first LLM on a custom dataset.

Let's get started.

The Big Question: To Fine-Tune or To RAG?

Imagine you have a brilliant, freshly graduated doctor. They have a vast, general knowledge of medicine (our pre-trained LLM). Now, you need them to work in a specialized cancer research lab. You have two ways to get them up to speed:

1. **The Library Approach (RAG):** You can give the doctor a key to a comprehensive library filled with the latest oncology research papers. Whenever a complex case comes up, they can go to the library, look up the relevant information, and then make a diagnosis.
2. **The Fellowship Approach (Fine-Tuning):** You can enrol the doctor in a multi-year oncology fellowship. They'll study thousands of specific cases, learn the nuances of the field, and internalize the knowledge. Over time, their brain will literally be rewired to think like an oncologist.

This is the core of the RAG vs. Fine-Tuning. Let's break down each approach.

Deep Dive into RAG

RAG is the library approach. You're not changing the model's brain; you're just giving it the right books to read at the right time.

When a user asks a question, the system first retrieves relevant documents from a knowledge base (like your company's wiki, a set of legal documents, or product manuals). Then, it stuffs that retrieved information into the prompt as context for the LLM and asks it to generate an answer based only on that context.

When to choose RAG:

1. **If your information sources change constantly**, RAG is perfect. You simply update your knowledge base, and the LLM has access to the new information instantly.
2. **When you need to eliminate hallucinations**, you can use RAG to force the model to base its answers on a provided text, dramatically increasing factuality.
3. **When you need citations and verifiability**, using RAG, you know exactly which documents were retrieved to generate an answer, and you can easily cite your sources.

But, there's a catch: RAG's performance is entirely dependent on the quality of its retriever. If the "librarian" can't find the right book, the "doctor" is useless. It can also be constrained by the model's context window size.

Deep Dive into Fine-Tuning

Fine-tuning is the "fellowship" approach. You're taking the pre-trained model and further training it on a smaller, curated dataset of examples. This process updates the model's internal weights, fundamentally changing its behaviour.

In fine-tuning, **you create a dataset of prompt-completion pairs** that exemplify the exact behaviour you want. For example, to teach it a specific JSON format, your dataset would have hundreds of examples of natural language requests and their correctly formatted JSON outputs. You then train the model on this data, nudging its billions of parameters to get better at this specific task.

When to choose fine-tuning:

1. **When you need to teach a new skill or style,** RAG is great for knowledge, but it can't teach a model how to behave. If you want a chatbot that speaks like a pirate, summarizes legal documents in plain English, or writes code in a very specific style, fine-tuning is the way to go. You are teaching it a new capability.
2. **For tasks where latency is critical** and the knowledge doesn't change often, fine-tuning "bakes" the information directly into the model. The model doesn't need to perform a separate retrieval step at inference time, making it faster.
3. If you're **working in a field with a highly specific vocabulary or syntax**, fine-tuning helps the model master that language.

The most powerful systems often combine both approaches. You might fine-tune a model to be an expert summarizer and then use RAG to provide it with the specific documents to summarize at runtime. This gives you the best of both worlds: a model with the right skills and the right knowledge.

The Efficiency Revolution: PEFT and LoRA

Okay, so you've decided to fine-tune. The first thing you'll realize is that even for a **small model with 7 billion parameters**, updating all its weights is a monumental task. A full fine-tune requires a beastly amount of VRAM; we're talking multiple A100 or H100 GPUs, which are far beyond the reach of most developers.

For a 7B parameter model, the weights alone (at 16-bit precision) take up 14 GB. But during training, you also need to store the gradients and optimizer states (like Adam), which can easily triple or quadruple that requirement to 50-80 GB of VRAM. **This is the barrier that kept fine-tuning an exclusive, big-tech game for years.**

This is where **PEFT (Parameter-Efficient Fine-Tuning)** is used by developers. It's a collection of brilliant techniques built on a simple, powerful idea: freeze the original model and only train a tiny number of new parameters.

Let's say your LLM is a giant, complex multi-story building. A full fine-tune is like trying to renovate the entire building at once, which is incredibly expensive and disruptive. PEFT is like adding a new, high-tech elevator system or a rooftop garden. You leave the core structure untouched and only add or modify small, strategic components.

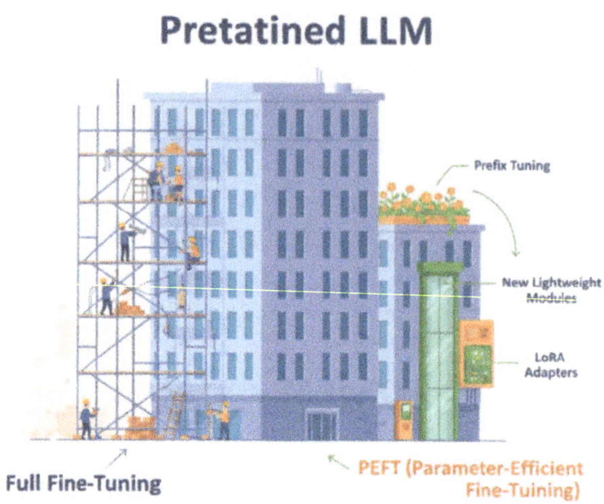

The star player in the PEFT family is LoRA (Low-Rank Adaptation).

Let's understand LoRA with our complex building analogy.

When we fine-tune, we're essentially calculating the "renovation plan" for the entire building, which means an update for every single parameter. This plan is represented by a massive matrix of changes, let's call it **ΔW**.

The key insight of LoRA is that this massive "renovation plan" **(ΔW)** is usually much simpler than it looks. It's low-rank, meaning it can be broken down into two much smaller, simpler plans.

Instead of learning the giant **ΔW** matrix directly, LoRA learns two small adapter matrices, **A and B**. When you multiply these two small matrices together **(B × A)**, you get a good approximation of the big renovation plan **(ΔW)**.

A Touch of Math

Let's say a weight **matrix W** in our model has a size of **d × k = 4096 × 4096**.

The update **matrix ΔW** would also be **4096 × 4096**, meaning we'd need to train over 16 million parameters for just this one layer!

LoRA introduces two smaller matrices:

1. **B**, with a size of **d × r** (e.g., **4096 × 8**)
2. **A**, with a size of **r × k** (e.g., **8 × 4096**)

Here, **r** is the rank, and it's a tiny number (like 8, 16, or 64).

The number of parameters we train is now just the sum of the parameters in **A and B: (4096 × 8) + (8 × 4096) = 65,536**

Compare that to the original 16,777,216 parameters.
That's roughly a 256× reduction in trainable parameters for this single layer!

This is the power of LoRA: we freeze the original **W** and only train **A and B.**

During inference, the final weight is simply calculated as: **W + B × A.**

The benefits are game-changing:

1. **Drastically Reduced VRAM:** You can now fine-tune large models on GPUs.
2. **Faster Training:** Fewer parameters mean faster training cycles.

Hands-on: Fine-Tuning a Small LLM with LoRA

Theory is one thing, but seeing a model's personality change after training is where your learning will really happen.

Our goal is to take the standard, general-purpose GPT-2 model and fine-tune it to perform a specific stylistic task: generating positive movie reviews. The base GPT-2 model knows about movies, but it has no specific opinion. We will teach it to be an optimistic movie critic.

This example is designed to be simple, fast, and run on a free Google Colab T4 GPU instance.

Step 1: Setup and Dependencies

First, let's install the essential libraries. We're using the Hugging Face ecosystem, which makes this process incredibly smooth:

1. **transformers:** For loading the base model and tokenizer.
2. **datasets:** To easily load and process our training data.
3. **peft:** The library that implements LoRA for us.
4. **trl:** Contains helpful tools for training, though we'll use the core Trainer here.
5. **accelerate:** Helps Hugging Face code run efficiently on any setup.

```
!pip install -q transformers datasets peft trl accelerate
```

Step 2: Load the Model and Tokenizer

We'll use GPT-2, a classic and reliable causal language model. It's small enough to train quickly but powerful enough to show a clear difference after fine-tuning. A critical step here is setting the tokenizer's padding token, which is necessary for batching our data together during training.

```
import torch
from transformers import AutoTokenizer, AutoModelForCausalLM
from datasets import load_dataset

# The model we want to fine-tune
model_name = "gpt2"

# Load the tokenizer
tokenizer = AutoTokenizer.from_pretrained(model_name)

# Set the padding token if it's not already set
if tokenizer.pad_token is None:
    tokenizer.pad_token = tokenizer.eos_token # Use the end-of-sequence token as the padding
token

# Load the model
model = AutoModelForCausalLM.from_pretrained(model_name)
```

Step 3: The Before Snapshot — Test the Base Model

Before we do any training, let's see how the original GPT-2 model behaves. We'll give it the beginning of a movie review and see how it completes it. This is our baseline.

```
# A prompt to test the model
prompt = "The movie started with a captivating scene that"

# Tokenize the input
inputs = tokenizer(prompt, return_tensors="pt")

# Generate a completion
# We're moving the model and inputs to the GPU if available
device = "cuda" if torch.cuda.is_available() else "cpu"
model.to(device)
inputs = inputs.to(device)

# Generate text
generate_ids = model.generate(inputs.input_ids, max_length=50)
response = tokenizer.decode(generate_ids[0], skip_special_tokens=True)

print("--- Base Model Response ---")
print(response)
```

```
--- Base Model Response ---
The movie started with a captivating scene that was so realistic that I thought it was real. I
was so excited to see the movie, but I was so disappointed. I was so disappointed that I
didn't even see the movie.
```

This is the behaviour we want to change.

Step 4: Load and Prepare the Dataset

We need data to teach our model the new style. We'll use the imdb dataset, filter it to only use positive reviews, and then format them into simple text prompts.

```
# Load the IMDB dataset
dataset = load_dataset("imdb", split="train")

# Filter for only positive reviews (label 1)
positive_reviews = dataset.filter(lambda example: example["label"] == 1)
```

```python
# To make this demo run quickly, let's just use a small subset of the data
small_dataset = positive_reviews.select(range(500)) # Using 500 examples for speed

# We need to format our examples into a single text string for the SFTTrainer
def format_review(example):
    # For this simple task, the text itself is our training data
    return {"text": "Review: " + example["text"] + " TL;DR: Positive."}

formatted_dataset = small_dataset.map(format_review)

print(formatted_dataset[0]['text'])
```

This will print the first review from our newly formatted dataset, showing the structure we'll use for training.

```
Review: I went and saw this movie last night after being coaxed to by a few friends of mine.
I'll admit that I was reluctant to see it because from what I knew of Ashton Kutcher he was
only able to do comedy. I was wrong. Kutcher played the character of Jake Fischer very well,
and Kevin Costner played Ben Randall with such professionalism. The sign of a good movie is
that it can toy with your emotions. This one did exactly that. The entire theater (which was
sold out) was filled with people who laughed, cried, and stood up and cheered for the rescues
made in the film. Such a great film that I will surely be buying on DVD. TL;DR: Positive.
```

Step 5: Configure and Apply LoRA

Now for the core of parameter-efficient fine-tuning. We'll create a LoRA configuration. The most important parameter is target_modules, which tells PEFT which layers of the model to apply the LoRA adapters to. For GPT-2, the attention layers are named c_attn.

```python
from peft import LoraConfig, get_peft_model

# Create the LoRA configuration
lora_config = LoraConfig(
    r=8,  # The rank of the update matrices.
    lora_alpha=16, # A scaling factor.
    target_modules=["c_attn"], # The specific layers to adapt.
    lora_dropout=0.1,
    bias="none",
    task_type="CAUSAL_LM"
)

# Wrap the base model with the PEFT model
peft_model = get_peft_model(model, lora_config)

# Let's see how many parameters we are actually training!
peft_model.print_trainable_parameters()
```

```
trainable params: 294,912 || all params: 124,734,720 || trainable%: 0.2364
```

This confirms that we are only training a tiny fraction of the model's parameters, which is why LoRA is so efficient.

Step 6: Set Up the Trainer and Train

This is where we prepare the model and data for the actual training loop. Unlike the simplified SFTTrainer, using the standard Trainer gives us more control. We'll explicitly tokenize the dataset and use a DataCollator to handle batching.

```
from transformers import TrainingArguments, Trainer, DataCollatorForLanguageModeling

# Some safety settings
peft_model.config.use_cache = False
tokenizer.padding_side = "right"
if tokenizer.pad_token_id is None:
    tokenizer.pad_token_id = tokenizer.eos_token_id
    peft_model.config.pad_token_id = peft_model.config.eos_token_id

# Tokenize the entire dataset
def tokenize_fn(batch):
    return tokenizer(
        batch["text"],
        truncation=True,
        padding="max_length",
        max_length=512,
    )

tokenized_ds = formatted_dataset.map(
    tokenize_fn,
    batched=True,
    remove_columns=formatted_dataset.column_names,
)

# The DataCollator handles batching and creating labels for us
data_collator = DataCollatorForLanguageModeling(
    tokenizer=tokenizer,
    mlm=False, # We're doing Causal LM, not Masked LM
)
```

```python
# Define the training arguments
training_args = TrainingArguments(
    output_dir="./gpt2-imdb-finetune",
    per_device_train_batch_size=2,
    gradient_accumulation_steps=2,
    learning_rate=2e-4,
    num_train_epochs=2,
    logging_steps=50,
    fp16=True, # Use mixed precision for speedup
    remove_unused_columns=False,
)

# Create the Trainer instance
trainer = Trainer(
    model=peft_model,
    args=training_args,
    train_dataset=tokenized_ds,
    data_collator=data_collator,
)


# And now, we train!
print("Starting training...")
trainer.train()
print("Training complete!")
```

As the model trains, you'll see a progress bar (as shown below) and the training loss being printed. The loss value should steadily decrease, showing that the model is learning.

[246/250 1:50:41 < 01:48, 0.04 it/s, Epoch 1.96/2]

Step	Training Loss
50	3.848900
100	3.746800
150	3.748400
200	3.672000

[250/250 1:52:57, Epoch 2/2]

Step	Training Loss
50	3.848900
100	3.746800
150	3.748400
200	3.672000
250	3.719800

```
Training complete!
```

Step 7: The After Snapshot — Test the Fine-Tuned Model

The above step will take some hours to complete. Once it's completed, we will use the same prompt as in Step 3:

```
print("\n--- Fine-Tuned Model Response ---")

# The trainer wraps the model, so we use trainer.model
fine_tuned_model = trainer.model

# Generate text using the fine-tuned model
generate_ids = fine_tuned_model.generate(inputs.input_ids, max_length=50)
response = tokenizer.decode(generate_ids[0], skip_special_tokens=True)

print(response)
```

Now, the response should be dramatically different. Instead of something generic, you'll get a completion that is clearly positive and has adopted the style of the movie reviews it was trained on.

```
--- Fine-Tuned Model Response ---
The movie started with a captivating scene that was both beautiful and touching. The acting
was superb and the story was very well told. I highly recommend this movie to anyone who loves
a good story. TL;DR: Positive.
```

Now, you've successfully altered the model's behaviour using LoRA. You now have a specialist model that is great at writing positive movie reviews, built upon the foundation of a generalist.

Summary

So, this chapter provided a guide to adapting general-purpose LLMs into specialized tools. It focuses on the critical decision between two primary adaptation methods and the modern techniques that make this process accessible.

RAG vs. Fine-Tuning: The Core Decision

1. **Retrieval-Augmented Generation (RAG):** Choose RAG when you need to inject external, factual, or rapidly changing knowledge into the model. It's like giving the model an open-book exam; it uses its reasoning on the information you provide. **Use it for tasks like Q&A over internal documents or customer support bots.**
2. **Fine-Tuning:** Choose fine-tuning when you need to change the model's fundamental behaviour, style, or output format. It's like teaching the model a new skill. **Use it to make the model adopt a specific persona, generate structured data like JSON, or learn a new language dialect.**

We, concluded this chapter with a hands-on guide demonstrating how to fine-tune a GPT-2 model using LoRA. By training it on a small dataset of positive movie reviews, the guide shows how to successfully change the model's default neutral tone to a consistently positive and stylistic one, proving the effectiveness of the technique.

Chapter 5
Generative AI for Images and Media

Welcome to one of the most visually stunning corners of the AI universe! If you've seen hyper-realistic portraits of people who don't exist, fantastical landscapes from the minds of machines, or artistic creations that blur the line between human and artificial creativity, you've witnessed the power of generative AI for images. This technology isn't just a novelty; it's revolutionizing everything from graphic design and entertainment to product prototyping and scientific visualization.

In this chapter, we'll start with the core concept that powers most modern image generation: **Diffusion Models**. Then, we'll go through the industry titans, **Stable Diffusion and DALL·E**. Finally, we'll build our very own text-to-image generator application from scratch.

Let's get started!

Understanding Diffusion Models: From Noise to Art

Let's say you are a sculptor. You will start with a rough, formless block of marble. With each chip and scrape, you will remove the excess, slowly revealing the beautiful statue hidden within.

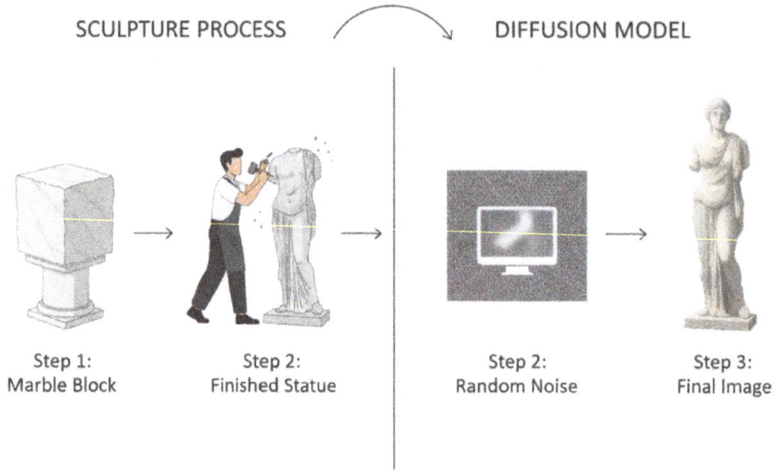

Diffusion models work in a surprisingly similar way, but instead of a block of marble, they start with a canvas of pure, random noise, like the static on an old TV screen.

How Diffusion Models Work?

At its heart, the diffusion process is a two-part process: first, you learn how to destroy an image, and then you use that knowledge to create a new one from scratch.

1. The Forward Process (The Destruction): Adding Noise

This is the "learning" phase. Imagine we take a beautiful, clear photograph, say, of a cat.

Now, we start adding a tiny bit of random, "Gaussian" noise to it. The image is now slightly fuzzy. We repeat this process, adding a little more noise at each step.

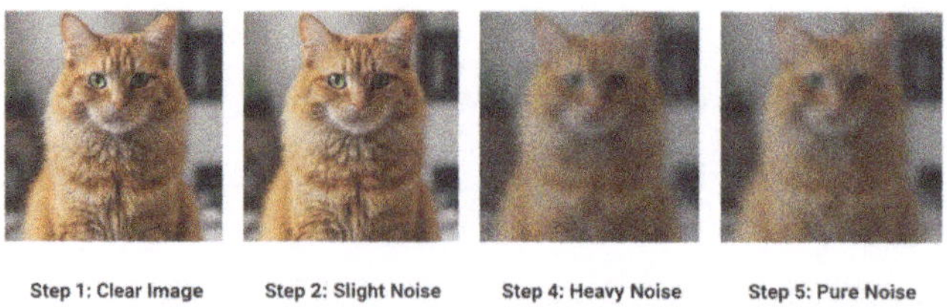

After hundreds or thousands of these small steps, the original cat photo is completely gone, replaced by a field of pure, indistinguishable static. It's just random noise.

This might seem counterintuitive.

Why would we want to destroy a perfectly good image?
Because in this process of controlled destruction, we've created a step-by-step recipe of how an image devolves into noise. This is the crucial information our AI model needs to learn. This forward process is fixed; we know exactly how much noise we add at each step.

2. The Reverse Process (The Creation): Denoising
This is where the image generation really happens. We train a powerful neural network (typically a U-Net architecture, which is excellent at image processing tasks) to do one thing: reverse the process.

We give the model one of the noisy images from our forward process (e.g., the image at step 350) and ask it: "What noise was added to get to this point?" The model's job isn't to guess the final, clean image directly. Instead, its sole focus is to predict the noise present in the image.

If the model can accurately predict the noise, we can simply subtract it from the image. By doing so, we take a tiny step backwards, from step 350 to step 349, making the image just a little bit clearer.

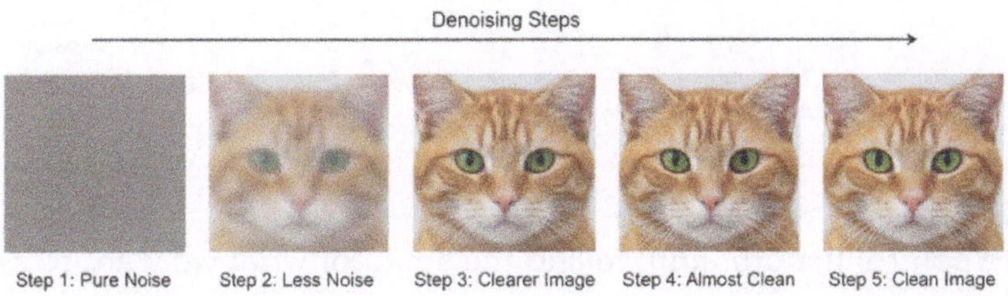

We repeat this over and over. We start with a completely random canvas of noise (the final step, T), feed it to our model, and ask it to predict the noise. We subtract that predicted noise, getting a slightly less noisy image. We take this new image, feed it back into the model, and repeat.

With each step, a coherent image slowly emerges from the static, just like our statue emerging from the marble. The final result is a brand-new, AI-generated image that has never existed before.

So, how does text fit in? (Text-to-Image Generation)

To guide this process, we give the model an extra piece of information at every step: a text prompt, like "a cat wearing a top hat."

This text is converted into a numerical representation (an embedding) by a text encoder model (like CLIP). This embedding acts as a "condition" or a guide.

At each denoising step, the model looks at both the noisy image and the text embedding. It learns to predict the noise in a way that will steer the final image toward the description in the text.

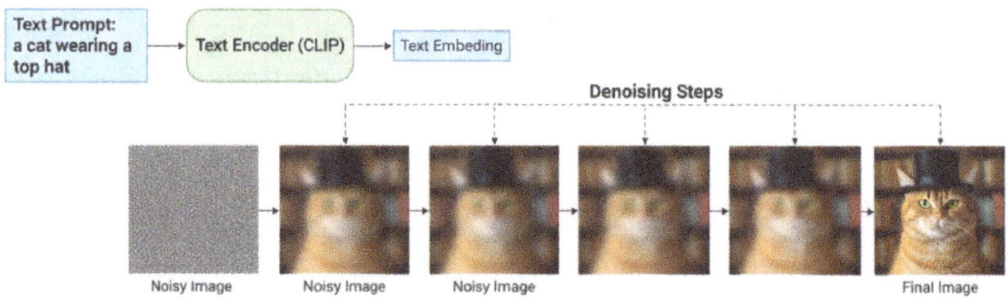

This is how we control the creation, telling the sculptor what we want to see.

The Mathematics Behind Diffusion Models

The forward process can be described as a Markov chain where we add Gaussian noise at each timestep **t** according to a variance schedule β_t.

An image at step **t**, denoted as x_t, is created from the image at the previous step x_{t-1}:

$$q(x_t \mid x_{t-1}) = N(x_t ; \sqrt{(1-\beta_t)} \times x_{t-1} , \beta_t I)$$

Here, N represents a normal (Gaussian) distribution.

All this equation says is that the new image x_t is the previous image x_{t-1}, slightly scaled down, with some noise added.

The β_t values are pre-defined and typically increase with **t**, meaning we add more noise in later steps.

The Reverse Process

The reverse process is the tricky part. Here, we need to learn the distribution $p\theta(x_{t-1} \mid x_t)$, where θ represents the weights of our neural network.

The network, $\epsilon\theta(x_t, t)$, is trained to predict the noise ϵ that was added to an original image x_0 to get the noisy version x_t.

The model is trained by minimizing a simple loss function, the mean squared error between the actual noise added and the noise predicted by our U-Net:

$$L = E_{t,x_0,\epsilon} [|| \epsilon - \epsilon\theta(x_t, t) ||^2]$$

In simple words, it means: for this noisy image x_t at this specific time **t**, tell me the noise ϵ that I need to remove.

Meet the Titans: Stable Diffusion and DALL·E

Now that we understand the core mechanics, let's look at two of the most influential models in this space. While both are text-to-image models, they have different architectures and philosophies.

Stable Diffusion

Stable Diffusion, first released in 2022, was a game-changer because it was made open-source, allowing anyone with a decent consumer GPU to run it. It's a Latent Diffusion Model (LDM).

Instead of performing the diffusion process on massive, high-resolution images (e.g., 512x512 pixels), which is computationally expensive, Stable Diffusion does it in a much smaller, compressed latent space. Here's how it works:

1. **Encoder:** A powerful Variational Autoencoder (VAE) takes the input image and compresses it from pixel space into a smaller latent representation. Think of this as creating a highly compressed ZIP file of the image's essential concepts, not just its pixels.
2. **Latent Diffusion:** The entire diffusion process we discussed earlier, adding noise and then iteratively denoising, happens in this compact and efficient latent space. This is the step where the text prompt guides the generation.
3. **Decoder:** Once the denoising is complete in the latent space, the VAE's decoder skillfully unpacks this latent representation back into a full-sized, high-resolution image.

This approach is brilliant because it dramatically reduces the computational power needed, making it possible to run on consumer hardware.

Working Example (with Hugging Face diffusers)

The diffusers library from Hugging Face makes it incredibly easy to use Stable Diffusion:

```
# Make sure you have the necessary libraries installed:
# pip install torch diffusers transformers accelerate
import torch
from diffusers import StableDiffusionPipeline

# This will download the model weights the first time you run it
pipe = StableDiffusionPipeline.from_pretrained(
    "runwayml/stable-diffusion-v1-5",
    torch_dtype=torch.float16
)
pipe = pipe.to("cuda") # Move the model to the GPU

# The text prompt
prompt = "a cinematic photograph of a lone astronaut discovering a glowing, alien forest on a distant planet"

# Generate the image
image = pipe(prompt).images[0]
# Save the image
image.save("astronaut_discovery.png")
```

Sample Output:

You do need a GPU-enabled system for image generation using diffusers.

DALL·E 3

DALL·E, developed by OpenAI, has always been a leader in quality and prompt understanding. The latest version, DALL·E 3, represents a significant leap forward, primarily due to its deep integration with a powerful Large Language Model (LLM) like GPT-4.

Key Feature: It Understands You, Really Understands You

The standout feature of DALL·E 3 is its uncanny ability to adhere to long, complex, and nuanced prompts. You can describe scenes with specific spatial relationships, multiple subjects, and detailed styles, and it often gets it right.

This is because, behind the scenes, your simple prompt is often expanded and enriched by an LLM. If you write, "an owl reading a book," the LLM might rewrite it into a more detailed prompt for the diffusion model, like:

"An illustrative, detailed image of a wise brown owl with large spectacles perched on a stack of leather-bound books, intently reading one of them by candlelight in a cozy, wood-paneled library."

This **prompt engineering** step helps the model generate images that are much more faithful to the user's intent.

Working Example (with the OpenAI API)

DALL·E 3 is primarily accessed via an API. You don't need it as a student.

If your company ever wanted you to use it, they would give you access to the API.

Now, let's look at an example of text-to-image generation using DALL·E 3!

```
# Make sure you have the openai library installed:
# pip install openai

import os
from openai import OpenAI

# It's best practice to set your API key as an environment variable
# client = OpenAI(api_key="YOUR_OPENAI_API_KEY")
client = OpenAI() # The client will automatically look for the OPENAI_API_KEY environment
variable

prompt = "An oil painting of a futuristic cityscape at sunset, in the style of Monet, with
flying cars leaving light trails."

try:
    response = client.images.generate(
        model="dall-e-3", # Specify the DALL-E 3 model
        prompt=prompt,
        n=1, # Number of images to generate
        size="1024x1024", # Available sizes for DALL-E 3
        quality="standard" # or "hd" for higher quality
    )

    image_url = response.data[0].url
    print(f"Image generated successfully! You can view it here: {image_url}")

except Exception as e:
    print(f"An error occurred: {e}")
```

Sample Output:

Hands-on: Generating Thumbnails and Visuals

Now, let's move beyond one-off image generation and build a practical workflow for creating consistent, on-brand visuals for a fictional blog called "AI Insights."

The Challenge: The Visual Content Treadmill (Case Study)
Professionally designed graphics are expensive and slow to procure. Stock photos are often generic and don't quite fit your message. This is where you, as an AI practitioner, have a massive advantage. We're going to use Stable Diffusion to become our own in-house graphic designer.

Our goal is to create visuals that are:

- **On-Brand:** They share a consistent style, color palette, and mood.
- **Relevant:** They accurately reflect the topic of the content.
- **Fast:** We can generate them in minutes, not hours or days.

As an AI Engineer, your task here is to build a tool for this company that can act as an in-house graphic designer.

Step 1: The Art of the Prompt - Defining a Visual Identity
Before we write any code or prompts, we must think like a designer. The key to consistency is to define a "visual identity" that we can translate into a master prompt.

For our "AI Insights" blog, let's define the identity:

1. **Style:** Minimalist vector art, clean lines, futuristic feel.
2. **Colour Palette:** A professional and modern mix of deep blue (#0A2342), electric cyan (#00FFFF), and white space.
3. **Mood:** Innovative, clean, intelligent, and approachable.
4. **Composition:** Often centred, with clear subjects and sometimes negative space for text overlays.

These human-language descriptors are the secret sauce. We can now translate them into keywords for our AI model.

Step 2: Crafting a "Master Prompt" Template

Instead of starting from scratch every time, we'll create a reusable prompt template.

This is the single most effective trick for maintaining brand consistency. Our master prompt template will look like this:

`"Minimalist vector art of [SUBJECT], professional blog thumbnail, futuristic and clean style, using a colour palette of deep blue and electric cyan, simple background, high resolution"`

The [SUBJECT] is a placeholder we'll replace for each new piece of content. The rest of the prompt acts as a set of powerful instructions that enforces our brand's visual identity on every image.

Step 3: Generating a Blog Post Thumbnail

Let's say we've written a new blog post titled:
"The Rise of AI Agents in Modern Business."

We need a thumbnail. Our subject is an "AI agent." How can we visualize that? Let's try "a smart robot brain processing data."

1. **Identify the subject:** a smart robot brain processing glowing data streams
2. **Insert into the master prompt:** "Minimalist vector art of a smart robot brain processing glowing data streams, professional blog thumbnail, futuristic and clean style, using a colour palette of deep blue and electric cyan, simple background, high resolution"
3. **Add Compositional Cues:** We know we'll want to add the blog title on top of the image later. So, let's ask the AI for some space. We'll add a crucial phrase: negative space at the top.

So, our final prompt will look something like this:

`"Minimalist vector art of a smart robot brain processing glowing data streams, professional blog thumbnail, futuristic and clean style, using a color palette of deep blue and electric cyan, simple background, negative space at the top, high resolution"`

Let's generate this using our Python script:

```
# Assuming 'pipe' is our loaded Stable Diffusion model from the previous example

prompt = "Minimalist vector art of a smart robot brain processing glowing data
streams, professional blog thumbnail, futuristic and clean style, using a color
palette of deep blue and electric cyan, simple background, negative space at the
top, high resolution"

# Using a negative prompt can help refine the output
negative_prompt = "photorealistic, 3d render, blurry, complex, text, watermark"

image = pipe(
    prompt,
    negative_prompt=negative_prompt,
    num_inference_steps=50,
    guidance_scale=8.0
).images[0]

image.save("ai_agents_thumbnail_raw.png")
```

You now have a production-ready, on-brand visual in a fraction of the time and cost it would normally take. Here's the output I got:

You might think that this hands-on exercise was less about code and more about the prompt. In Generative AI, writing the prompt is as important as building the model was in Machine Learning.

In our hands-on example, the Python code to call the Stable Diffusion API was relatively straightforward. The real creative and technical leverage, the difference between a generic, messy image and a stunning, on-brand visual, was entirely in the prompt.

Make sure to take prompt writing seriously if you want to build a career in GenAI and LLMs.

Summary

In this chapter, we covered how modern AI image generation works by explaining the core concept of Diffusion Models, which learn to create detailed images by reversing a process of adding noise to a picture. We explored the industry's leading tools, the open-source Stable Diffusion and OpenAI's highly intuitive DALL·E 3.

The hands-on section provided a practical workflow for a common real-world task: generating consistent, on-brand thumbnails and visuals for blogs and social media.

Chapter 6 Multimodal Generative AI

Have you ever tried to describe a hilarious meme to a friend over the phone? It's a struggle, right? You use your words to paint a picture ("Okay, so this cat is sitting at a table..."), describe the text overlay, and maybe even mimic the tone of the caption. In that moment, you are seamlessly translating between modalities: vision, language, and context. You're performing an incredibly complex cognitive task that, until very recently, was pure science fiction for computers.

Welcome to the world of **multimodal AI**, the frontier where models learn to see, read, and listen, not as separate skills, but as interconnected senses. For the longest time, AI was like a specialist with tunnel vision. A language model was a brilliant wordsmith but was blind. A computer vision model could identify a thousand objects, but couldn't read the story they were a part of.

Multimodal generative AI shatters those walls. It's about building models that understand the world more like we do, a rich, interwoven tapestry of sights, sounds, and text.

This chapter is your guide to understanding how multimodal GenAI works, from the core concepts to building your very own system that can look at a picture and answer your questions about it.

Let's get started.

How AI Developed a "Common Sense" for Different Data

At its heart, the challenge of multimodal AI is a translation problem. A computer sees an image as a grid of pixel values (RGB numbers) and text as a sequence of characters or tokens.

These are fundamentally different languages. How do you teach a machine that the pixel grid representing a fluffy, four-legged animal is conceptually linked to the token sequence d-o-g?

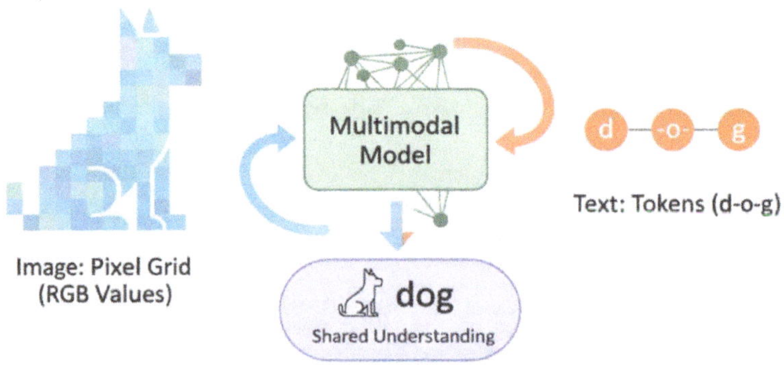

The Universal Library of Concepts

Imagine a magical library where ideas, not book titles or painting names, are the organizing principle. On one shelf, you find a photograph of a golden retriever, a poem about loyalty, and the audio of a happy bark. They are all different formats (modalities), but they represent the same core concept.

This "universal library" is the core intuition behind modern multimodal AI. The goal isn't to convert an image into text, but to convert both the image and the text into a common, shared representation, a universal language of meaning. **In machine learning, we call this a shared embedding space.**

An embedding is just a vector, a list of numbers, that captures the essence of a piece of data. The idea behind this is that in this shared space, vectors for conceptually similar items are mathematically close. The vector for a picture of an apple is near the vector for the word "apple."

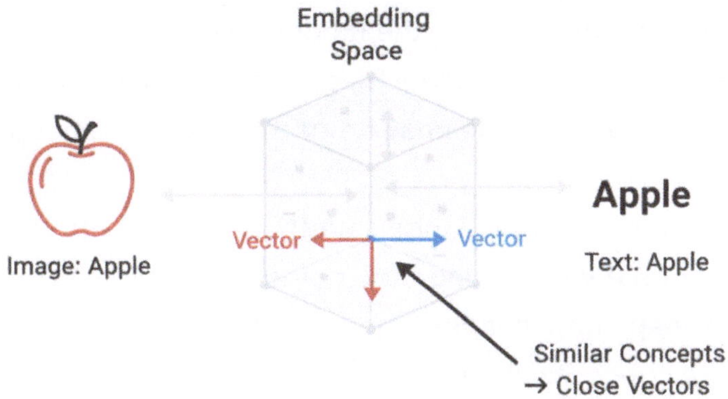

The Mathematics

So, how do we create this shared space? We use a clever architecture, famously demonstrated by models like CLIP (Contrastive Language-Image Pre-training).

1. **The Image Encoder:** This is a neural network, often a Vision Transformer (ViT) or a classic Convolutional Neural Network (CNN), that has been trained to look at an image and distil its visual features into a single vector, or embedding. It learns to recognize textures, shapes, objects, and their relationships.
2. **The Text Encoder:** This is another neural network, typically a Transformer (like the ones used in BERT or GPT), that reads a piece of text and condenses its semantic meaning into a vector.
3. **The Matchmaker (Contrastive Learning):** This is where the learning happens. The model is trained on a massive dataset of (image, caption) pairs scraped from the internet. For each pair:

The image encoder creates an image embedding ($\mathbf{v_i}$).

The text encoder creates a text embedding ($\mathbf{v_t}$).

The model's goal is to make these two vectors as similar as possible. Mathematically, it tries to maximize the cosine similarity (a measure of how much two vectors point in the same direction) between a matching image and text pair.

Simultaneously, for that same image, the model is shown captions from other images in the batch (these are called "negative" samples). It then tries to minimize the similarity between the image and these incorrect captions.

This process of pulling the right things together, pushing the wrong things apart, is called **contrastive learning**. By doing this millions of times, the encoders learn to map both images and text into a beautifully structured shared space where concepts align.

The New Wave: Natively Multimodal Giants like Gemini and GPT-4V

Models like CLIP were a breakthrough, but they still had two separate brains, one for vision and one for language, that learned to communicate. The next generation, including Google's Gemini and OpenAI's GPT-4V, takes a more profound approach: they are natively multimodal.

How These Models Work: A Single Stream of Thought

Instead of two specialists, imagine a single, powerful brain that was designed from birth to process a continuous stream of information, regardless of whether it's a word or a visual.

This is the core idea. These models don't just associate images with text; they read them as part of the same input sequence.

But, how? By turning images into a kind of vocabulary.

The model first breaks an image down into a grid of smaller patches. Each patch is then converted into a numerical vector, or an "image token." From the model's perspective, a prompt like:

`What is the main subject of this photo? [image]`

is transformed into a single, unified sequence of tokens:

`[token_what] [token_is] [token_the] ... [token_photo?] [image_token_1] [image_token_2] ... [image_token_N]`

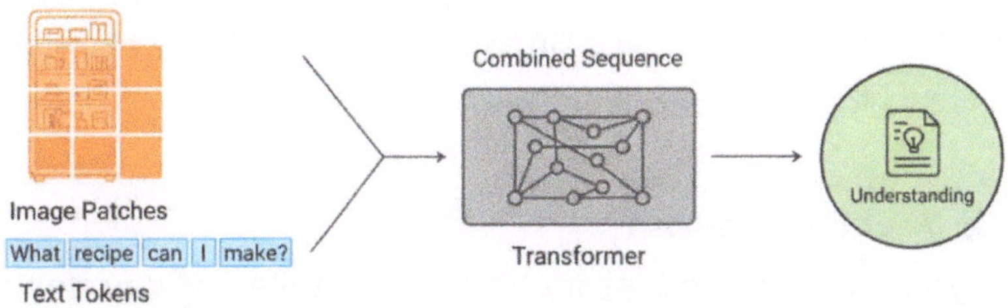

The Transformer architecture, which is brilliant at finding patterns in sequences, doesn't care that some tokens came from words and others from image patches. It processes the entire sequence, allowing it to perform incredibly sophisticated reasoning that intertwines visual information and linguistic instructions.

This is how it can look at a picture of a refrigerator's contents and suggest a recipe, or explain why a visual meme is funny.

It's not just seeing and reading; it's understanding.

Hands-on: Building a Visual Question Answering (VQA) System

Now, let's build something! We're going to create a VQA system, a program that takes an image and a natural language question and provides an answer. This is a classic multimodal task that beautifully demonstrates the power of these models.

We'll use the Hugging Face transformers library and a powerful pre-trained model called **BLIP (Bootstrapping Language-Image Pre-training)**. BLIP is an excellent choice because it was specifically designed for vision-language tasks that require this kind of deep, joint understanding.

Step 1: Setting Up Your Environment

First, make sure you have the necessary libraries installed. If you don't, open your terminal and run this command. We need transformers for the model, torch as the backend framework, and Pillow for image manipulation.

pip install transformers torch Pillow

Step 2: Create a Python File

Let's write a Python script. Create a file named **vqa_app.py** and follow along. We'll go through it block by block.

Imports and Model Loading

First, we need to import the necessary components. We need PIL to open our image, requests to fetch it from a URL, and the specific BLIP processor and model classes from transformers:

```python
import requests
from PIL import Image
from transformers import BlipProcessor, BlipForQuestionAnswering

# Load the processor and model from the Hugging Face Hub.
# The processor prepares the data for the model (image preprocessing and text
tokenization).
# The model is the actual pre-trained network that will answer our question.
processor = BlipProcessor.from_pretrained("Salesforce/blip-vqa-base")
model = BlipForQuestionAnswering.from_pretrained("Salesforce/blip-vqa-base")

print("Model and processor loaded successfully!")
```

Here, the processor is a crucial helper. It knows exactly how to resize and normalize an image and how to convert our question into tokens that the BLIP model understands.

Prepare the Image and Question

Now, let's find an image and come up with a question. We'll use a photo of a human with a dog:

```python
# Let's use an image from the web
img_url = 'https://storage.googleapis.com/sfr-vision-language-
research/BLIP/demo.jpg'
raw_image = Image.open(requests.get(img_url, stream=True).raw).convert('RGB')

# Define the question you want to ask about the image
question = "How many people are in the picture?"
```

This is the image we are using looks like.

Process the Inputs

This is where the processor helps in this task. We feed it the raw image and the question, and it bundles them up into a format ready for the model:

```
# The processor combines the image and text into the model's expected format.
# `return_tensors="pt"` tells it to return PyTorch tensors.
inputs = processor(raw_image, question, return_tensors="pt")

print("Inputs prepared for the model.")
```

Generate the Answer

With our inputs ready, we pass them to the model and call the generate() method. This is the moment of inference, the model looks at the image, reads the question, and formulates an answer:

```
# Feed the inputs to the model to get the output
out = model.generate(**inputs)

print("Model has generated an answer.")
```

Decode and Print the Result

The model's output (out) is a sequence of token IDs. To make it human-readable, we use the same processor to decode these IDs back into a string:

```
# Decode the generated token IDs back into a text string
answer = processor.decode(out[0], skip_special_tokens=True)

print("\n---\n")
print(f"Question: {question}")
print(f"Answer: {answer}")
print("\n---")
```

You should see an output like this:

```
---

Question: How many people are in the picture?
Answer: 1

---
```

Now, you've just built a fully functional Visual Question Answering system. Try it with different images and questions.

Ask about colours, objects, actions, or the relationships between things. You'll be amazed at the level of detail these models can perceive.

Summary

This chapter introduced multimodal generative AI, which enables models to understand and integrate various data types like text, images, and audio. We covered the core principle of a shared embedding space, where different modalities are translated into a common mathematical language, allowing models like CLIP to connect visual and textual concepts.

We then explore advanced, natively multimodal models such as Gemini and GPT-4V, which process images and text as a single, unified input for more sophisticated reasoning.

The chapter culminates in a hands-on guide to building a Visual Question Answering (VQA) system using the BLIP model, demonstrating how to make an AI that can look at an image and answer questions about it.

Chapter 7 Introduction to AI Agents

If you've been following the GenAI space, you've seen the incredible power of Large Language Models. They can write poetry, summarize dense legal documents, and even generate code. But for all their brilliance, a standalone LLM is like a genius brain in a jar; it can think, but it can't do. It can tell you how to book a flight, but it can't actually book it for you.

This is where AI Agents come in. Agents are the next evolutionary step, giving that brilliant brain hands, feet, and a connection to the outside world.

They transform the LLM from a passive knowledge-provider into an active problem-solver. In this chapter, we're going to understand what agents are, explore their core architecture, and build one from scratch.

Let's get started.

From Thinkers to Doers: What Are AI Agents?

At its core, an AI Agent is a system that can perceive its environment, make decisions, and take actions to achieve a specific goal.

Think about how you operate in the real world. Let's say you have a goal ("I'm hungry, I want pizza").

You perceive your environment (check the fridge, see no pizza). You make a plan (find a pizzeria online, place an order). You take actions (use your phone to open a delivery app, click buttons). Finally, you get feedback from the environment (the app confirms your order, the pizza arrives).

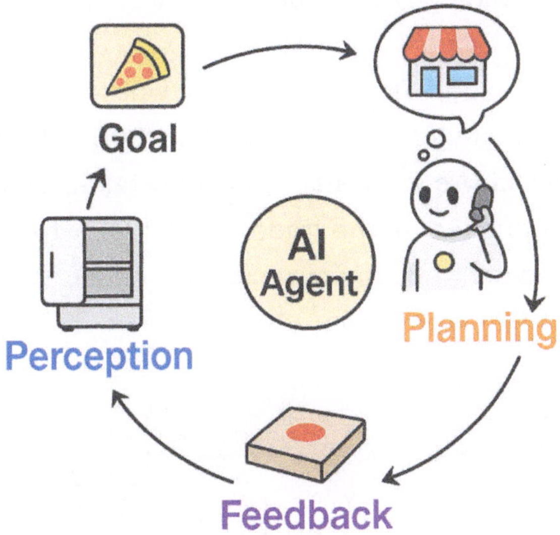

An AI Agent works on the same principle. It's an autonomous entity that doesn't just respond to a prompt; it actively works to get a job done.

The Key Difference: LLMs vs. Agents

The most common point of confusion is understanding how an agent differs from a powerful LLM like GPT-4 or Llama 3. The distinction is simple but profound.

An **LLM is a reasoning engine**. Its primary function is to process a text input and generate a text output. It's a master of language, knowledge, and logic, but its interaction with the world is confined to that text-in, text-out interface.

An AI Agent is an action engine which uses an LLM (not compulsory though) as its brain. The LLM is the core reasoning component, but the agent system surrounds it with capabilities for action, perception, and memory.

In simple words, an LLM is like a brilliant economics professor. You can ask her, "Based on current market trends, is now a good time to invest in tech stocks?" She will give you a well-reasoned, insightful, and comprehensive essay on the topic. But she can't buy the stock for you.

But an AI Agent is like an expert financial advisor who consults that same professor. The advisor listens to your goal ("Invest $5,000 in tech"), uses the professor's reasoning (the LLM's analysis), and then takes action by using tools like a brokerage API to execute the trade, a calculator to determine the number of shares, and then confirms the purchase via email.

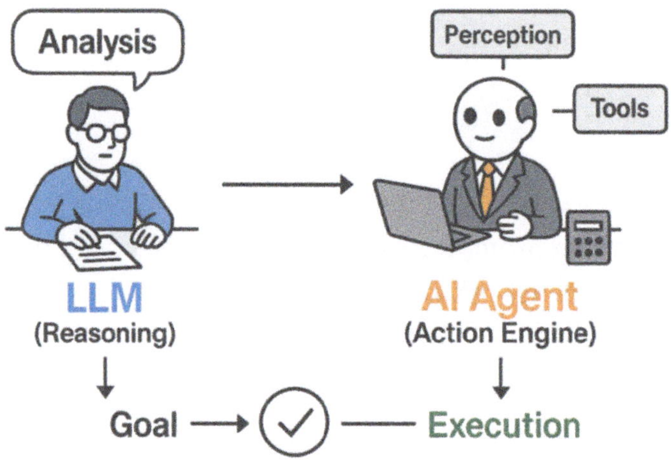

The agent completes the loop from thought to action.

The Core Architecture of an Agent

Most AI agents, from simple bots to highly complex systems, are built around four fundamental components that work together in a continuous cycle. Let's break down this architecture.

1. The Agent (The Brain)

This is the heart of the system, the central decision-maker.
In modern agents, the brain is almost always an LLM. Its job is to:

1. **Understand the Goal:** Deconstruct the user's high-level objective. A query like **"How's my company's stock doing today compared to our main competitor?"** isn't a single question; it's a goal that requires multiple steps.
2. **Create a Plan:** Break down the goal into a sequence of smaller, actionable steps.
3. **Make Decisions:** At each step, the agent decides what to do next. Most importantly, it decides if it needs help from the outside world by using a Tool.

Most AI agents, from simple bots to highly complex systems, are built around four fundamental components that work together in a continuous cycle. Let's break down this architecture.

2. Tools (The Hands)

Tools are external programs, functions, or APIs that give the agent the ability to interact with the world and gather information that isn't in its pre-trained knowledge. The agent's LLM brain doesn't know how to execute code or browse the web, but it's smart enough to know when it needs to and which tool to use.

Common examples of tools include:

1. **Web Search:** API to search Google or Bing.
2. **Code Interpreter:** A sandboxed environment to execute Python or other code for calculations, data analysis, or plotting.
3. **Database Access:** Functions to query a SQL or NoSQL database.
4. **APIs:** Any external API, such as a weather API, a stock market data provider, or an internal company API.

An agent's power is directly proportional to the quality and variety of the tools it can use.

3. Memory (The Notebook)

For an agent to perform any task that requires more than one step, it needs memory. Memory allows the agent to retain context, learn from its actions, and avoid repeating mistakes.

1. **Short-Term Memory:** This is the agent's working memory, often just the history of the current conversation or task. It helps the agent remember the output of a previous step to inform the next one. For example, after finding a stock price with a tool, it needs to remember that price to use it in the final summary.
2. **Long-Term Memory (Advanced):** In more sophisticated agents, this allows for storing information across sessions. This could be user preferences ("I prefer summaries in bullet points") or knowledge gained from past tasks ("The API for XYZ often fails, so I should have a backup plan").

4. Environment (The World)

The environment is where the agent operates and takes action. It provides the context and the feedback loop.

For a software agent, the environment could be a user's operating system (to manage files), a web browser (to scrape websites), a database or a server, or a user's chat interface.

The agent takes an action via a tool, which changes the state of the environment. The agent then perceives this new state, and the cycle continues until the goal is achieved.

This loop—Perceive → Think (Plan) → Act—is the fundamental rhythm of every AI Agent.

Hands-on: Building a Rule-Based Web Research Assistant

Alright, let's get our hands dirty. We're going to build our first agent, piece by piece. The goal is to create a simple assistant that can take a topic, search for it on Wikipedia, and give us a neat summary.

This exercise is designed to be run in a Google Colab notebook. We'll create a separate cell for each logical step, so you can run them one by one and understand what's happening.

Step 1: Setting Up the Environment

First things first, we need to install the necessary libraries. This is always the starting point for any project. We'll install everything quietly (-q) to keep our notebook clean.

Run this cell in your Colab notebook:

```
# Install the required Python libraries
!pip install wikipedia transformers torch sentencepiece -q
```

The **sentencepiece** we installed here is a tokenizer that is required by the specific model we'll be using. A tokenizer essentially chops up our text into pieces that the model can understand.

Step 2: Building Our First Tool - The Wikipedia Searcher

An agent needs tools to interact with its environment. Our agent's environment is the web (specifically, Wikipedia), so its first tool will be a search function.

This function will take a topic, search Wikipedia for it, and grab the full content of the page. We'll also add some error handling, because the real world is messy, searches can fail or be ambiguous:

```
import wikipedia

def search_wikipedia(topic: str) -> str:
    """
    This is our first tool. It searches for a topic on Wikipedia
    and returns the content of the page.
    """
    print(f"🛠 Using Tool: search_wikipedia(topic='{topic}')")
    try:
        # We use wikipedia.page() to get the full page object
        # auto_suggest=False prevents it from guessing a different topic
        page = wikipedia.page(topic, auto_suggest=False, redirect=True)
        return page.content
    except wikipedia.exceptions.PageError:
        return f"Error: Sorry, I could not find a Wikipedia page for '{topic}'."
    except wikipedia.exceptions.DisambiguationError as e:
        # This happens when a topic is too broad (e.g., "Apple")
        return f"Error: '{topic}' is ambiguous. Did you mean one of these {e.options[:5]}"
    except Exception as e:
        return f"An unexpected error occurred: {e}"
```

Here, we've created a function, search_wikipedia, that acts as a self-contained tool. The agent will be able to call this function by name. Notice how we've wrapped the core logic in a try...except block. A robust agent needs robust tools that can handle failure gracefully instead of crashing.

Here's how you can test this function:

```
# Let's test our new tool!
test_content = search_wikipedia("Reinforcement learning")
print(f"\nTool Test Output (first 200 chars): {test_content[:200]}...")
```

Step 3: Building Our Second Tool - The Text Summarizer

Getting a giant wall of text from Wikipedia isn't very useful. We need another tool to distil that information into a concise summary.

For this, we'll use a pre-trained model from the Hugging Face Hub called **t5-small**. It's lightweight, fast, and great for this kind of task.

This cell will first download and load the model and its tokenizer. This might take a minute the first time you run it.

```
from transformers import T5ForConditionalGeneration, T5Tokenizer

# --- Load Model and Tokenizer (this happens only once) ---
print("Loading summarization model (t5-small)... This may take a moment.")
model_name = "t5-small"
try:
    tokenizer = T5Tokenizer.from_pretrained(model_name)
    model = T5ForConditionalGeneration.from_pretrained(model_name)
    print("Model and tokenizer loaded successfully.")
except Exception as e:
    print(f"Error loading model: {e}")
    model = None # Set to None if loading fails
```

Now, we'll define the summarize_text function:

```
# --- Define the Summarization Tool ---
def summarize_text(text: str) -> str:
    """
    This is our second tool. It uses a T5 model to summarize text.
    """
    if model is None:
        return "Error: Summarization model is not available."

    print(f"🛠 Using Tool: summarize_text(...)")

    # T5 models require a prefix for different tasks. For summarization, it's "summarize: ".
    text_to_summarize = "summarize: " + text

    # 1. Tokenize: Convert the text into a format the model understands
    inputs = tokenizer.encode(text_to_summarize, return_tensors="pt",
    max_length=512, truncation=True)
```

```
#continued...
    # 2. Generate: Ask the model to generate the summary
    summary_ids = model.generate(
        inputs,
        max_length=150,      # The longest the summary can be
        min_length=40,       # The shortest it can be
        length_penalty=2.0,  # Encourages the model not to use too many words
        num_beams=4,         # A technique for generating higher-quality text
        early_stopping=True
    )

    # 3. Decode: Convert the generated output back into human-readable text
    summary = tokenizer.decode(summary_ids[0], skip_special_tokens=True)
    return summary
```

Here's what we did in this step:

1. **Model Loading:** We download the t5-small model and its corresponding tokenizer. We only do this once to be efficient.
2. **The summarize_text function:** This is our second tool. It follows a standard **Tokenize >> Generate >> Decode** pattern common in NLP.
3. **model.generate():** This is where we pass our tokenized text to the model and let it generate a new sequence of tokens representing the summary. The parameters we've set help guide the model to produce better results.

Step 4: Designing the Agent's Brain

Now that we have our tools, we need an Agent to orchestrate them. Our agent's brain will be a simple Python class with a run method.

This method will contain the hard-coded logic for our research task: first search, then summarize. This demonstrates the core **Think >> Act >> Observe loop** in a very explicit way.

```
class WebResearchAgent:
    def __init__(self):
        self.memory = {} # A simple dictionary to store results between steps

    def run(self, research_topic: str) -> str:
        """
        The main execution loop of the agent.
        """
        print(f"\n🤖 Agent starting job for topic: '{research_topic}'")
```

```
# continued...
        # --- STEP 1: SEARCH ---
        print("\n[Thinking] I need to find information on the web for this topic. I'll use the search_wikipedia tool.")
        article_content = search_wikipedia(research_topic) # Action
        self.memory['raw_article'] = article_content      # Store in memory

        # Observation
        if "Error:" in article_content:
            print(f"[Observation] The search tool failed. Aborting job.")
            return article_content # Return the error message

        print(f"[Observation] Successfully fetched the article. It's {len(article_content)} characters long.")


        # --- STEP 2: SUMMARIZE ---
        print("\n[Thinking] The article is too long to read. I need to summarize it. I'll use the summarize_text tool.")
        summary = summarize_text(article_content) # Action
        self.memory['summary'] = summary           # Store in memory

        # Observation
        print("[Observation] The text has been summarized.")

        print("\nAgent job finished.")
        return summary

print("WebResearchAgent class defined.")
```

Here's what's happening in this step:

1. **WebResearchAgent class:** We've encapsulated all the agent's logic in a class. This is good practice and will allow us to create more complex agents later.
2. **self.memory:** This simple dictionary is our agent's short-term memory. It stores the result of the search (raw_article) so it can be used in the next step.
3. **The run method:** This is the core logic. **Notice the print statements prefixed with [Thinking] and [Observation].** This explicitly shows the agent's thought process. It decides what to do, calls a tool, observes the result, and then decides the next step.

Step 5: Putting It All Together and Running the Agent!

We have all the components: tools and an agent brain. Now it's time to bring it all to life. The final block of code will create an instance of our agent, ask you for a topic, and then kick off the run method:

```python
# --- Main Execution Block ---
agent = WebResearchAgent()

# Get user input
topic = input("Hello! What would you like me to research today? ")

# Run the agent
final_summary = agent.run(topic)

# Display the final result in a nice format
print("\n\n==================================================")
print("       ✨ Here is your research summary: ✨")
print("==================================================")
print(f"\nTopic: {topic}\n")
print(final_summary)
print("\n==================================================")
```

```
Hello! What would you like me to research today? Pizzas

🤖 Agent starting job for topic: 'Pizzas'

[Thinking] I need to find information on the web for this topic. I'll use the search_wikipedia
tool.
🛠 Using Tool: search_wikipedia(topic='Pizzas')
[Observation] Successfully fetched the article. It's 19688 characters long.

[Thinking] The article is too long to read. I need to summarize it. I'll use the
summarize_text tool.
🛠 Using Tool: summarize_text(...)
[Observation] The text has been summarized.

 Agent job finished.


==================================================
      ✨ Here is your research summary: ✨
==================================================

Topic: Pizzas

the term pizza was first recorded in 997 AD, in a Latin manuscript from the southern italian
town of Gaeta, in lazio, on the border with Campania. in 2009, Neapolitan pizza was registered
with the European Union as a traditional speciality guaranteed (TSG) dish. in 2017 the art of
making Neapolitan pizza was included on UNESCO's list of intangible cultural heritage.

==================================================
```

You've just built and run your first AI Agent. You gave it a high-level goal, and it autonomously used a sequence of tools to achieve it. You saw it, think, act, and observe.

Summary

This chapter introduced AI Agents, moving beyond passive Large Language Models to create autonomous systems that can achieve goals.

Key Takeaways

Agents vs. LLMs: While an LLM is a brilliant text-generation engine, an AI Agent is a complete system that uses an LLM as its brain to perceive, think, and act within an environment. The key difference is the ability to take autonomous actions to complete a task.

The Agentic Loop: Agents operate on a continuous loop of **Think → Act → Observe.** They assess the goal and current state (think), use a tool to perform an action (act), and then analyze the result of that action (observe) to decide what to do next.

We also built a practical, rule-based Web Research Assistant. This simple agent demonstrated the core concepts by autonomously using a Wikipedia search tool to gather information and a Hugging Face summarization tool to process it, completing its research goal from a single user prompt.

Chapter 8
Building Multi-Agent Systems

In the last chapter, we focused on what a single, powerful AI agent can do. We've armed it with tools, given it memory, and taught it how to reason. But what happens when the problem is too complex, too multifaceted for one agent to handle alone? The same thing that happens in human organizations: we build a team.

In this chapter, we're diving into multi-agent systems. This is where you level up from being an agent trainer to a team architect.

You'll learn how to design systems where multiple specialized AI agents collaborate, delegate, and even compete to solve complex problems more effectively than any single agent ever could.

We'll explore the core concepts that make these systems tick, and then we will build a practical, hands-on project using one of the most popular frameworks today, CrewAI.

Let's get started.

Cooperative and Competitive AI Agents

Before we build a team, we need to understand the team's dynamics. In the world of AI agents, interactions broadly fall into two categories: cooperative and competitive. Think of this as the difference between a soccer team and two rival companies.

Imagine a professional soccer team. The striker's goal is to score. The midfielder's goal is to move the ball forward and create opportunities. The defender's goal is to prevent the other team from scoring. While their individual roles are different, they all share a single, overarching objective to win the game.

The striker celebrates when the defender makes a great tackle, and the defender cheers when the striker scores. Their individual successes are intertwined and contribute to a collective victory.

This is a cooperative system. The agents, or players, work together, sharing information (calling out plays) and resources (the ball) to achieve a common goal. It's a non-zero-sum game; the team's success is a shared reward.

Now, picture two rival smartphone companies, let's call them Apple and Samsung. Both want to dominate the market. If Apple sells one million more phones this quarter, that's one million fewer phones Samsung might have sold. Apple's success comes at the direct expense of Samsung's, and vice versa.

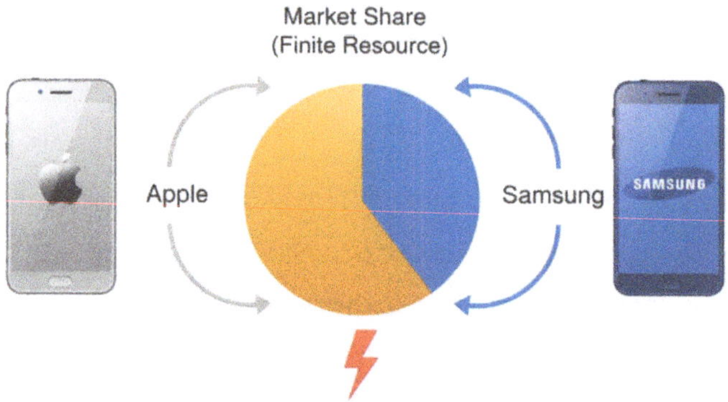

They are in a competitive or adversarial relationship. They don't share their product roadmaps or marketing strategies. Instead, they react to each other's moves, trying to out-innovate and out-market the other to capture a larger share of a finite resource (market share). This is a classic zero-sum game (or close to it).

The Mathematics

While we don't need to dive into formal game theory, understanding the core concepts will be helpful.

Cooperative Agents (Non-Zero-Sum Game)

In these scenarios, the total payoff or reward is not fixed. Agents can work together to increase the total pie before deciding how to slice it.

The mathematical models here often involve maximizing a collective utility function: $\mathbf{U(a_1, a_2, ..., a_n)}$, where the **actions** $\mathbf{(a_i)}$ of all agents contribute to a shared outcome. The goal is to find a set of actions that makes everyone better off.

Competitive Agents (Zero-Sum Game)
In a pure zero-sum game, one agent's gain is precisely another agent's loss.

The total reward is constant. If agent A gains **+x**, agent B must gain **−x**.

This is modelled using concepts like the **minimax algorithm**, where each agent tries to minimize the maximum possible loss its opponent can inflict.

Think of Chess or Go, there's a finite outcome (win, lose, or draw), and one player's advantage is the other's disadvantage.

Most real-world applications you'll build, especially in business and research automation, will involve cooperative agents. You'll design agents with specialized skills that work together to write code, conduct market analysis, or plan a travel itinerary.

The Pillars of Collaboration

For a team of agents to function as more than just a collection of individuals, they need mechanisms to collaborate. These mechanisms are surprisingly human-like: **they need to delegate tasks, use the right tools, and talk to each other.**

Task Delegation: The Art of Knowing Who Does What
Imagine you're managing a project. You wouldn't ask your graphic designer to write the backend database code. You delegate tasks based on expertise. Multi-agent systems work the same way.

A manager or orchestrator agent receives a high-level goal, let's say, to produce a market research report on the electric vehicle industry. It then breaks this down into sub-tasks:

1. "Find the latest news and market data on EVs." **Assigns to a Research Agent.**
2. "Analyze the collected data for key trends and competitors." **Assigns to a Data Analysis Agent.**
3. "Summarize the findings into a well-structured report." **Assigns to a Writer Agent.**

This process of breaking down a problem and assigning the pieces to the most suitable agent is task delegation. The output of one agent's task often becomes the input for the next, creating a workflow or pipeline.

Tool Usage: Giving Your Agents Superpowers

We've touched on this before, but in a multi-agent context, tools become even more critical. You don't just give one agent a Swiss Army knife; you give each specialist agent their specific, high-powered toolkit.

For example, a Research Agent might be equipped with tools to search the web (e.g., DuckDuckGo Search, Google Serper API), access academic papers (e.g., ArXiv API), or browse specific websites. A Code Writer Agent would have tools to write files to disk, read files, and execute terminal commands to test its code. Whereas a Financial Agent could have tools to fetch real-time stock prices or analyze financial statements.

By equipping agents with distinct tools, you are defining and reinforcing their specialized roles within the system.

Communication: The Lifeblood of Teamwork

Agents can't work in a vacuum. They need to share information, results, and status updates. This is where communication comes in.

How do agents talk? It's not quite like a Slack channel, but the principle is similar. Communication is typically managed by the underlying framework through a shared state or context. Communication between AI Agents include:

1. **Passing Context:** The simplest form is a sequential pipeline. The Research Agent finishes its task, and its final output (a block of text with all the data) is passed directly as the starting context for the Writer Agent.
2. **Shared Scratchpad:** More complex systems might use a shared memory or scratchpad. Agents can write their findings to this central location, and other agents can read from it. This allows for more dynamic, non-linear collaboration, where an agent can access information from multiple other agents.
3. **Conversational Exchange:** In frameworks like AutoGen, agents engage in a literal turn-by-turn conversation. One agent speaks (generates a response), and this response is broadcast to other agents, who then decide how to react. This mimics a human brainstorming session.

An Effective collaboration is a mix of all three: a clear delegation of tasks, the right tools for the job, and a seamless way to communicate results.

Multi-Agent Frameworks

Building a multi-agent system from scratch is a heavy lift.

Thankfully, we have powerful frameworks that handle the complex plumbing of communication, state management, and task execution. Let's look at three of the most popular players: **CrewAI, AutoGen, and LangGraph.**

Feature	CrewAI	AutoGen	LangGraph
Core Metaphor	A hierarchical crew of agents with specific roles.	A conversation between agents in a chat group.	A state machine graph where nodes are actions.
Best For	Structured, process-oriented workflows.	Complex, dynamic problem-solving and conversational simulations.	Building cyclical, stateful, and highly controllable agentic loops.
When to Use It	You want to automate a business process with clear, distinct roles.	You need agents to debate, critique, and refine ideas together.	You need loops, human-in-the-loop validation, or complex conditional logic.

In short:

1. **Use CrewAI** when you think of your problem as a corporate team or an assembly line.
2. **Use AutoGen** when you think of your problem as a committee meeting or a brainstorming session.
3. **Use LangGraph** when you think of your problem as a flowchart.

Hands-on: Building a Multi-Agent Research Team with CrewAI

Now, let's build something. Before starting, I'll recommend you to go through the documentation of CrewAI. Just to let yourself know what exactly it is.

What will we build Today?

Our goal is to create a powerful two-agent crew that can research any given topic and write a blog post about it. For this first build, we're going to do something interesting: we will not provide our agents with any external tools, like a web browser (as assessing them will be expensive for you as a student).

Instead, we'll rely on the vast internal knowledge stored within the Large Language Model itself. This is a great way to understand the core concepts of agent roles and task handoffs.

Our team will consist of:

1. **A Senior Researcher:** This agent's job is to search its own internal knowledge base (the LLM's trained data) to find key information.
2. **A Tech Content Strategist:** This agent will take the researcher's organized notes and write a polished, human-readable blog post.

Step 1: Setting Up Your Environment

First, let's get our workspace ready. The beauty of this approach is its simplicity. You only need CrewAI and a way to run a local LLM. We'll use the fantastic Ollama for that.

First, Install Ollama. If you haven't already, head over to ollama.com and download the application for your operating system. It's the easiest way to get powerful open-source models running on your own machine.

Next, Download a Model. Once Ollama is installed and running, open your terminal and pull a powerful model. We'll use **Llama 3**, which has a vast knowledge base. Execute this command on the terminal:

ollama pull llama3

You will see the installation like this:

(venv) (base) amankharwal@Amans-MacBook-Pro multiagents % **ollama pull llama3**

```
pulling manifest
pulling 6a0746a1ec1a: 100% ██████████ 4.7 GB
pulling 4fa551d4f938: 100% ██████████ 12 KB
pulling 8ab4849b038c: 100% ██████████ 254 B
pulling 577073ffcc6c: 100% ██████████ 110 B
pulling 3f8eb4da87fa: 100% ██████████ 485 B
verifying sha256 digest
writing manifest
success
```

Next, **install CrewAI** in your Python virtual environment:

pip install crewai

And that's it! No extra tools or community packages are needed for this version.

Step 2: Building and Directing Your Crew

Now, let's write the Python script. Create a file named **main.py,** and let's get started.

First, we will configure the LLM:

```python
from crewai import Agent, Task, Crew, Process
# We will use CrewAI's new simplified LLM integration
from crewai.llm import LLM

# --- Part 1: Configure the LLM ---
# This tells CrewAI how to connect to our local Ollama model.
# The format 'ollama/<model_name>' is the standard way.
llm = LLM(model="ollama/llama3")
```

Now, we will define our Agents. The first agent will be the researcher:

```
# --- Part 2: Define Your Agents (The Team Members) ---
# An agent is like an employee with a specific job description.

# Agent 1: The Researcher
researcher = Agent(
    role='Senior Researcher',
    goal='Uncover groundbreaking technologies and trends in {topic}',
    backstory=(
        "You distill the most relevant and compelling insights from your vast knowledge
base. "
        "You identify key trends, explain why they matter, and keep things concise."
    ),
    verbose=True,  # This allows us to see the agent's thinking process
    allow_delegation=False,  # This agent works alone on its tasks
    llm=llm  # Assign the LLM to this agent
)
```

Now, we will define the second agent. The second agent will the the writer:

```
# Agent 2: The Writer
writer = Agent(
    role='Tech Content Strategist',
    goal='Craft a compelling and insightful blog post on {topic}',
    backstory=(
        "You turn complex technical points into engaging, accessible writing. "
        "You love clarity, flow, and practical takeaways for the reader."
    ),
    verbose=True,
    allow_delegation=False,
    llm=llm
)
```

Now, we will define the tasks for our Agents. The task for the first agent will be to research the topic:

```
# Task 1: Research the Topic
research_task = Task(
    description=(
        "Identify the top 3-5 most significant trends in {topic} this year. "
        "For each trend, provide 2-3 bullet points with key facts or implications. "
        "Your final answer MUST be a concise, well-structured list."
    ),
    expected_output='A bulleted list summary of the top 3-5 trends in the specified
topic.',
    agent=researcher  # Assign this task to the researcher agent
)
```

Now, we will define the task 2. This task will be assigned to the writer to write a blog post using the information gathered from the researcher:

```
# Task 2: Write the Blog Post
write_task = Task(
    description=(
        "Using the research findings provided, write a ~500-word blog post in
Markdown. "
        "Include: a catchy title, a brief introduction, one section per trend with
clear subheadings, "
        "and a short conclusion with a forward-looking takeaway."
    ),
    expected_output='A ~500-word blog post formatted in Markdown.',
    agent=writer,  # Assign this task to the writer agent
    context=[research_task]  # *** THIS IS THE MAGIC! ***
                             # It tells this task to use the output of research_task
as its starting point.
)
```

Now, we will build a crew using our agents. The Crew is the final team ready to execute the plan:

```
crew = Crew(
    agents=[researcher, writer],
    tasks=[research_task, write_task],
    process=Process.sequential,  # Tasks will be executed one after another
    verbose=True  # We want to see the crew's progress
)
```

Now, let's write the driver code:

```
if __name__ == "__main__":
    # Define the topic we want to research
    topic = "AI in Healthcare"

    # Start the crew's work!
    result = crew.kickoff(inputs={'topic': topic})

    # Print the final result
    print("\n\n########################")
    print("## Here is the final result:")
    print("########################\n")
    print(result)
```

Step 3: Running the Crew

Save your **main.py** file. **Make sure your Ollama application is running in the background.** Now, execute the script from your terminal:

python main.py

Your terminal will come alive with the inner monologue of your AI crew. Because we set verbose=True, CrewAI shows us the play-by-play. Here's what you will see in the output:

```
(venv) (base) amankharwal@Amans-MacBook-Pro multiagents % python main.py
──────────────────── Crew Execution Started ────────────────────

  Crew Execution Started
  Name: crew
  ID: 4cc01786-ef1c-4c08-93e7-5d37401334ca
  Tool Args:


🚀 Crew: crew
└── 📋 Task: baad134f-bcd0-4364-bd8e-2638e1edee0a
    Status: Executing Task...
──────────────────── 🤖 Agent Started ────────────────────

  Agent: Senior Researcher

  Task: Identify the top 3-5 most significant trends in AI in Healthcare this year.
  For each trend, provide 2-3 bullet points with key facts or implications. Make it
  concise and well-structured.


🚀 Crew: crew
└── 📋 Task: baad134f-bcd0-4364-bd8e-2638e1edee0a
    Status: Executing Task...

──────────────────── ✅ Agent Final Answer ────────────────────

  Agent: Senior Researcher

  Final Answer:
  **Top Trends in AI in Healthcare (2023)**

  • **1. Explainable AI (XAI) in Medical Imaging**

          + XAI enables physicians to understand how AI-driven diagnostic tools arrive
  at their conclusions, improving trust and reducing errors.
          + This trend is particularly significant in medical imaging, where accurate
  diagnosis relies heavily on image interpretation.
          + XAI can also help identify biases in AI systems, ensuring more equitable
  decision-making.
```

```
🚀 Crew: crew
└── 📋 Task: baad134f-bcd0-4364-bd8e-2638e1edee0a
    Assigned to: Senior Researcher
    Status: ✅ Completed
╭──────────────────────────── Task Completion ────────────────────────────╮
│                                                                          │
│  Task Completed                                                          │
│  Name: baad134f-bcd0-4364-bd8e-2638e1edee0a                              │
│  Agent: Senior Researcher                                                │
│  Tool Args:                                                              │
│                                                                          │
│                                                                          │
╰──────────────────────────────────────────────────────────────────────────╯

🚀 Crew: crew
├── 📋 Task: baad134f-bcd0-4364-bd8e-2638e1edee0a
│   Assigned to: Senior Researcher
│   Status: ✅ Completed
└── 📋 Task: 797fece6-f66d-4c04-8302-592a1e6b3cbd
    Status: Executing Task...
╭──────────────────────────── 🤖 Agent Started ────────────────────────────╮
│                                                                          │
│  Agent: Tech Content Strategist                                          │
│                                                                          │
│  Task: Using the research findings provided, write a ~500-word blog post in Markdown.
│  Include: a catchy title, brief intro, one section per trend with clear subheadings,
│  and a short conclusion with a forward-looking takeaway.                 │
│                                                                          │
╰──────────────────────────────────────────────────────────────────────────╯
```

Next, you will see a blog post in the end as the final result. Now, you've just successfully built and managed your first multi-agent system!

You defined specialized roles, created a clear workflow, and orchestrated a seamless handoff of information between agents. This foundational skill is the key to automating incredibly complex digital workflows.

Summary

In this chapter, you've leapt from a single-agent operator to a multi-agent team architect.

We started by exploring the dynamics of agent teams: cooperative systems (like our research crew), where agents share a common objective, and competitive systems, where agents work against each other. We saw that successful collaboration hinges on three pillars: task delegation, tool usage, and agent-to-agent communication.

In the end, we built a practical, hands-on research crew using CrewAI. You learned how to define specialized agents (a Researcher and a Writer), assign them distinct tasks, and, most critically, enable them to collaborate by passing information from one agent to the next using the context parameter. You now have the foundational skills to automate complex, end-to-end workflows by building teams of specialized AI agents.

Chapter 9
Deploying GenAI Systems

You've built agents. You've mastered RAG. You've finetuned models. Now, for the most important part: how do you let someone use it?

A model sitting in a Jupyter Notebook is a fascinating experiment. A model deployed as an application is a tool.

This chapter is all about closing that gap, moving from model.predict() to a live, interactive, and robust application.

In this chapter, we will talk about creating interactive web UIs for your models and the core principles you must carry forward into your professional career.

Let's get started.

Streamlit: The Data Scientist's Best Friend

Streamlit is for data scientists and ML engineers who need to build a web app and hate web development (HTML, CSS, JavaScript). It lets you build a surprisingly complex, interactive web UI using nothing but Python.

Streamlit works on a **script-as-app model**. It re-runs your Python script from top to bottom every time a user interacts with a widget (like clicking a button or moving a slider). It's incredibly fast for building internal tools, demos, and dashboards.

Implementation Example:

Let's say we want to wrap our crewai script from the last chapter. Think of your main.py file as the engine of a car. This Streamlit script is the dashboard and pedals, the user interface that lets someone actually drive the car without needing to be a mechanic. So, let's start by creating a new file: **app_streamlit.py.**

Step 1: Imports

```
# create a new file in the same directory of main.py from last chapter.
# Name this file as: app_streamlit.py
import streamlit as st
from main import crew # Assuming your crew setup is in main.py
```

This is the standard way to import the Streamlit library.

Step 2: Page Setup

```
st.set_page_config(page_title="AI Agent Blog Writer", layout="centered")
st.title("🤖 Your AI Agent Crew")
st.write("Give me a topic, and my AI crew will research and write a blog post for you.")
```

st.set_page_config(...) sets the metadata for the browser tab. It gives it a title ("AI Agent Blog Writer") and tells Streamlit to use a nice, centred layout.

st.title(...) and st.write(...) simply render text on the page—a main title (<h1>) and a paragraph (<p>) of instructions for the user.

Step 3: Initializing Memory (Session State)

```
# Use a session state to hold the result
if 'result' not in st.session_state:
    st.session_state.result = ''
```

This is the single most important concept in Streamlit.

It re-runs your entire script from top to bottom every time a user interacts with a widget (like clicking a button).

It means if we just saved our blog post to a normal variable like my_result = ..., it would be erased on the very next re-run. The user would see the post for a split second, and then it would vanish.

st.session_state is a special dictionary that persists across re-runs. It's the app's short-term memory. This code block says, "If our memory doesn't have a 'result' key in it yet, create one and set it to an empty string."

This ensures our app has a place to store the blog post, and it won't be lost.

Step 4: Drawing the User Inputs

```
topic = st.text_input("Blog Post Topic:", placeholder="e.g., 'AI in Healthcare'")
```

This command draws an interactive text input box on the page.

Step 5: The Go Button and Core Logic

```
if st.button("Generate Blog Post 🚀"):
    if topic:
        with st.spinner("Crew is researching and writing... This may take a
moment..."):
            # Kick off the crew
            inputs = {'topic': topic}
            result = crew.kickoff(inputs=inputs)
            # Extract the actual text (CrewAI returns an object)
            if hasattr(result, 'output'):
                st.session_state.result = result.output  # new versions of CrewAI

            elif isinstance(result, dict) and 'output' in result:
                st.session_state.result = result['output']
            else:
                st.session_state.result = str(result)


        st.success("Blog post generated!")
    else:
        st.error("Please enter a topic.")
```

This if block is where all the action happens. The code inside only runs in the single re-run that happens when the user clicks the **"Generate Blog Post" button.**

Step 6: Displaying the Result

```
# Display the result (conditionally)
if st.session_state.result:
    st.markdown("---")
    st.subheader("Your Generated Blog Post:")
    st.markdown(st.session_state.result)
```

This block of code is at the end of the script. It runs every single time the page re-runs. Because our display logic is based on session_state, the generated post will stay on the screen even as the user interacts with other (potential) widgets, until they generate a new one.

After this, run your file using: **python app_streamlit.py**

You will see an output like this:

Your AI Agent Crew

Give me a topic, and my AI crew will research and write a blog post for you.

Blog Post Topic:

AI in Healthcare

Generate Blog Post 🚀

Crew is researching and writing... This may take a moment...

Final Output:

Generate Blog Post 🚀

Blog post generated!

Your Generated Blog Post:

"Unlocking the Power of AI in Healthcare: Top Trends Transforming Clinical Care"

The healthcare industry has witnessed tremendous advancements this year, with Artificial Intelligence (AI) playing a crucial role in transforming clinical care. From improving patient outcomes to reducing administrative burdens, AI is revolutionizing the way healthcare providers deliver care. In this post, we'll explore the top trends shaping the future of AI in Healthcare.

NLP for Clinical Documentation: Revolutionizing Reporting

Natural Language Processing (NLP) is transforming clinical documentation by allowing clinicians to dictate reports, reducing transcription errors and costs. This trend has significant implications for improved accuracy and speed of clinical reporting, enhanced patient safety through timely and accurate

Your Journey Doesn't End Here

And with that, we're at the end of our book.

If you've made it this far, building and tinkering along the way, you are no longer just a learner. You are a practitioner. You have the complete, end-to-end toolkit to build the next generation of intelligent systems.

But I have to be honest with you. This is, without a doubt, the fastest-moving field in human history.

The models I used in the code example in this book might be outdated by the time you're reading this. A new agentic architecture that blows all previous benchmarks away might have just dropped on arXiv this morning.

This can feel intimidating. It's like trying to drink from a firehose.

So, my final words to you aren't about another AI Agent. They're about a mindset. Your goal is not to know everything. That's impossible. Your new, primary skill is learning how to learn and developing high-quality filters.

1. Don't Chase Hype. Understand First Principles.
You don't need to use every new model that's trending. But you do need to understand why it's trending. Is it a new architecture (like Mixture of Experts)? Is it a breakthrough in context length? Is it a new data-generation technique?

The models will change, but the first principles you learned in this book will not.

2. Build, Build, Build (and Build Some More)

Reading a paper is theory. Watching a YouTube video is entertainment. Building is where learning happens.

The only way to make these abstract concepts stick is to get your hands dirty. Your code will break. Your prompts will fail. Your agent will get stuck in a loop. This is the work. Every error message is a lesson. Every project you build, no matter how small, is a brick in your foundation.

Take the agent you built in Chapter 7 and swap its brain for that new open-source model. Try to make your RAG system from Chapter 3. Answer five questions at once. Build a Streamlit app for it. This hands-on, practical application is what separates an engineer from a theorist.

3. You Are Now a GenAI Systems Engineer

The new, durable role in the industry is the GenAI Systems Engineer. This is a person who understands the entire stack:

1. **The Data (RAG, vector DBs)**
2. **The Model (APIs, open-source, fine-tuning)**
3. **The Logic (agentic frameworks, orchestration)**
4. **The Application (Streamlit, APIs, deployment)**

You are no longer just a model person or a data person. You are a systems person. This book was designed to make you exactly that.

Final Words

You started this journey to learn about GenAI, LLMs, and AI Agents. I hope that you're finishing it not just with a set of new skills, but with a new sense of possibility.

These tools are the most powerful creative and intellectual force multipliers ever invented. They are not a replacement for human ingenuity. They are a partner. They are a mirror for our own intelligence and a motor for our own ambitions.

You have the skills. You have the hands-on experience. You know how to build the brain and the body.

Thank you for joining me on this journey. I can't wait to see what you create.

Go build it.

-Aman Kharwal